Stopwatch

Student's Book & Workbook

1

Simon Brewster

Richmond

Richmond
58 St Aldates
Oxford
OX1 1ST
United Kingdom

Stopwatch Student's Book Level 1

First Edition: January 2016
ISBN: 978-607-06-1238-1

Publisher: Justine Piekarowicz
Editorial Team: Daniel Altamirano, Suzanne Guerrero, Kimberly MacCurdy, Joep van der Werff
Art and Design Coordinators: Karla Avila
Design: Karla Avila
Layout: Erick López
Pre-Press Coordinator: Daniel Santillán
Pre-Press Team: Susana Alcántara, Virginia Arroyo
Cover Design: Karla Avila
Cover Photograph: © **Thinkstock.com** Ryan McVay / Photodisc (young man breakdancing)

Illustrations: Karla Avila pp. 16, 17, 24; Tomas Benitez pp. 45, 46; Luis Montiel pp. 20, 21; Berenice Muñiz pp. 32, 33, 70, 71, 100, 101; Ismael Vásquez pp. 11, 28, 29, 30, 31, 39, 52, 58, 59, 67, 73, 79, 91, 102, 103, 114, 126, 127, 139, 142, 146, 152

Photographs: © **Shutterstock.com:** Brendan Howard p. 36 (gymnastics), Aspen Photo p. 36 (basketball), LaiQuocAnh p. 42 (bottom right), Dan Breckwoldt p. 42 (top left), testing p. 48 (dancers), paul prescott p. 48 (bottom right), ryabuhina p. 48 (holi festival), Don Mammoser p. 49 (flute player), Songquan Deng p. 52 (bottom left), Bikeworldtravel p. 52 (top left), Tupungato p. 52 (red car), R.M. Nunes p. 52 (bottom right), Radiokafka p. 52 (India), julie deshaies p. 60 (mobile home), Quick Shot pp. 62-63, Quick Shot p. 63 (top), B Brown p. 64 (rustic), kavalenkau p. 65 (top), Zeynep Demir p. 72 (center), Boris-B p. 73 (bottom left), haak78 p. 76 (top right), Dainis Derics p. 76 (top center), Sandratsky Dmitriy p. 102 (bottom), Supannee Hickman (Osaka, Japón) p. 103, xuanhuongho (Vietnam) pp. 104-105, Ekaterina Bykova p. 119 (bottom right), FashionStock.com p. 150 (bottom center), NorGal p. 153 (Levi's), CLChang p. 154 (top center), Christopher Halloran p. 157 (center right)
© **Thinkstock.com:** manaemedia p. 26 (center left), robtek p. 26 (left), Julian Finney p. 46 (bottom left)
© **XINHUA/LANDOV:** Xinhua/Liu Changlong (school class) pp. 34-35

Images used under license from © **Shutterstock.com** and © **Thinkstock.com**.

Printed in Brazil by Forma Certa Gráfica Digital
Lote: 788939
Cod: 292712381

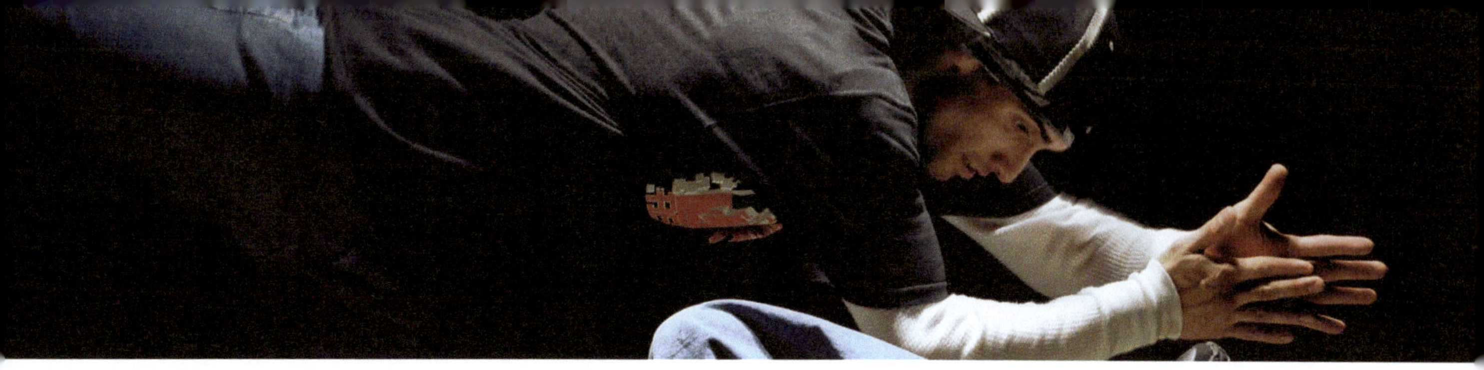

Contents

Scope and Sequence

Unit	Vocabulary	Grammar	Skills
0 What's your name?	The alphabet; Numbers 0-100; Colors; Instructions; Days, months and years	Parts of speech: verbs and nouns; Subject pronouns; *Can*	**Listening:** Understanding instructions
1 What is family?	**Family Relationships:** aunt, brother, cousin, daughter, father (dad), grandfather (grandpa), grandmother (grandma), grandparent, mother (mom), nephew, niece, parent, sister, son, uncle	Demonstratives; Possessive adjectives; Possessive *'s*; Verb *be*	**Reading:** Thinking about what you know **Writing:** Making a poster **Project:** Making an infographic
2 How do you learn?	**School Places:** art room, auditorium, bathroom, cafeteria, classroom, computer lab, gymnasium (gym), laboratory (lab), library, music room **School Subjects:** chemistry, geography, math (mathematics), technology, P.E. (physical education / gym class), physics, history, science, biology	Indefinite articles; Verb *have;* Prepositions of place: *under, in, next to, on*	**Listening:** Thinking about the topic **Writing:** Making a class schedule **Project:** Making a *Perfect School* collage
3 Where are you from?	**Countries and Nationalities:** Australia / Australian, Brazil / Brazilian, China / Chinese, Egypt / Egyptian, France / French, Greece / Greek, India / Indian, Italy / Italian, Japan / Japanese, Peru / Peruvian, Thailand / Thai, The United Kingdom (The UK) / British, The United States (The US) / American, Turkey / Turkish	Verb *be;* *Can*	**Reading:** Reading in steps **Speaking:** Presenting a city or town **Project:** Making a country profile
4 What is home?	**Rooms:** bathroom, bedroom, dining room, kitchen, laundry room, living room, closet **House Objects:** bed, chair, dryer, refrigerator (fridge), shower, sink, sofa, stove, table, television (TV), toilet, washer	*There is / are;* *Where;* Prepositions of place: *between, in front of, on, in, next to* Short answers	**Listening:** Looking at photos and making predictions **Reading:** Reading about statistics **Project:** Designing a home

Unit	Vocabulary	Grammar	Skills
5 What's your routine?	**Routines:** brush my teeth, do homework, get dressed, go to bed, go to school, eat breakfast / lunch / dinner, take a shower, wake up **Time Expressions:** six o'clock (six a.m. / p.m.), six (oh) five, a quarter past six, half past six (six thirty), a quarter to seven	Adverbs of frequency; Present simple	**Reading:** Reading a timetable **Listening:** Thinking about questions other people will ask you **Project:** Making an agenda
6 How important is technology to you?	**Technology Collocations:** check e-mail, listen to music, make phone calls, make a video, play games, send messages, share photos, shop online, surf the Internet, take photos, watch movies **E-mail:** compose, delete, print, reply, save	Frequency expressions; Question words	**Reading:** Using key words **Writing:** Writing search terms for a search engine **Project:** Making a technology infographic
7 What are you wearing?	**Clothing:** blouse, boots, coat, dress, hat, jacket, jeans, pajamas, pants, sandals, scarf (scarves), shoes, shorts, skirt, socks, sweater, tie, T-shirt **Adjectives:** casual, cheap, comfortable, elegant, expensive, popular, useful **Prices**	Present continuous	**Listening:** Listening for detail **Writing:** Using adjectives **Project:** Making VIP profiles
8 What do you love doing?	**Vacation Activities:** cook, get a tan, go climbing, go shopping, go snorkeling, go surfing, go swimming, go waterskiing, lift weights, play miniature golf	Likes and dislikes; *Let's*	**Listening:** Listening for large numbers **Reading:** Identifying similarities and differences **Project:** Making a free-time-activities survey

0

What's your name?

Unit 0

1 Listen and repeat the letters. (track 1)

2 Classify the letters.

rhyme with A: (A) (J) ( )

rhyme with B: (B) ( ) ( ) (E) ( ) ( ) ( ) (V) (Z)

sound like F: (F) (L) ( ) (N) ( ) ( )

other letters: (H) (I) ( ) (Q) ( ) (U) ( ) ( )

3 Listen and write the number words. (track 2)

0 →	zero	7 →	____
1 →	____	8 →	____
2 →	____	9 →	____
3 →	____	10 →	____
4 →	____	11 →	____
5 →	____	12 →	____
6 →	____		

4 Pronounce the letters to decode the number words.

0. 13 — t h (etʃ) irt e (i) en
1. 14 — ___ (ɛf) ___ (o) ur ___ (ti) een
2. 15 — f ___ (aɪ) ftee ___ (ɛn)
3. 16 — ___ (ɛs) i ___ (ɛks) teen
4. 17 — s ___ (i) ___ (vi) ente ___ (i) n
5. 18 — ei ___ (dʒi) h ___ (ti) een
6. 19 — ___ (ɛn) ___ (aɪ) net ___ (i) en
7. 20 — t ___ ("double" yu) ent ___ (waɪ)

The Alphabet

the letter → pronounced...

A	→ e
B	→ bi
C	→ si
D	→ di
E	→ i
F	→ ɛf
G	→ dʒi
H	→ etʃ
I	→ aɪ
J	→ dʒe
K	→ ke
L	→ ɛl
M	→ ɛm
N	→ ɛn
O	→ o
P	→ pi
Q	→ kyu
R	→ ar
S	→ ɛs
T	→ ti
U	→ yu
V	→ vi
W	→ "double" yu
X	→ ɛks
Y	→ waɪ
Z	→ zi

Guess What!

Where 0 is included in a phone number, it is pronounced "oh." For example: 237-0980 is two-three-seven-oh-nine-eight-oh.

1 min **5 Think Fast!** Spell your name and say your phone number.

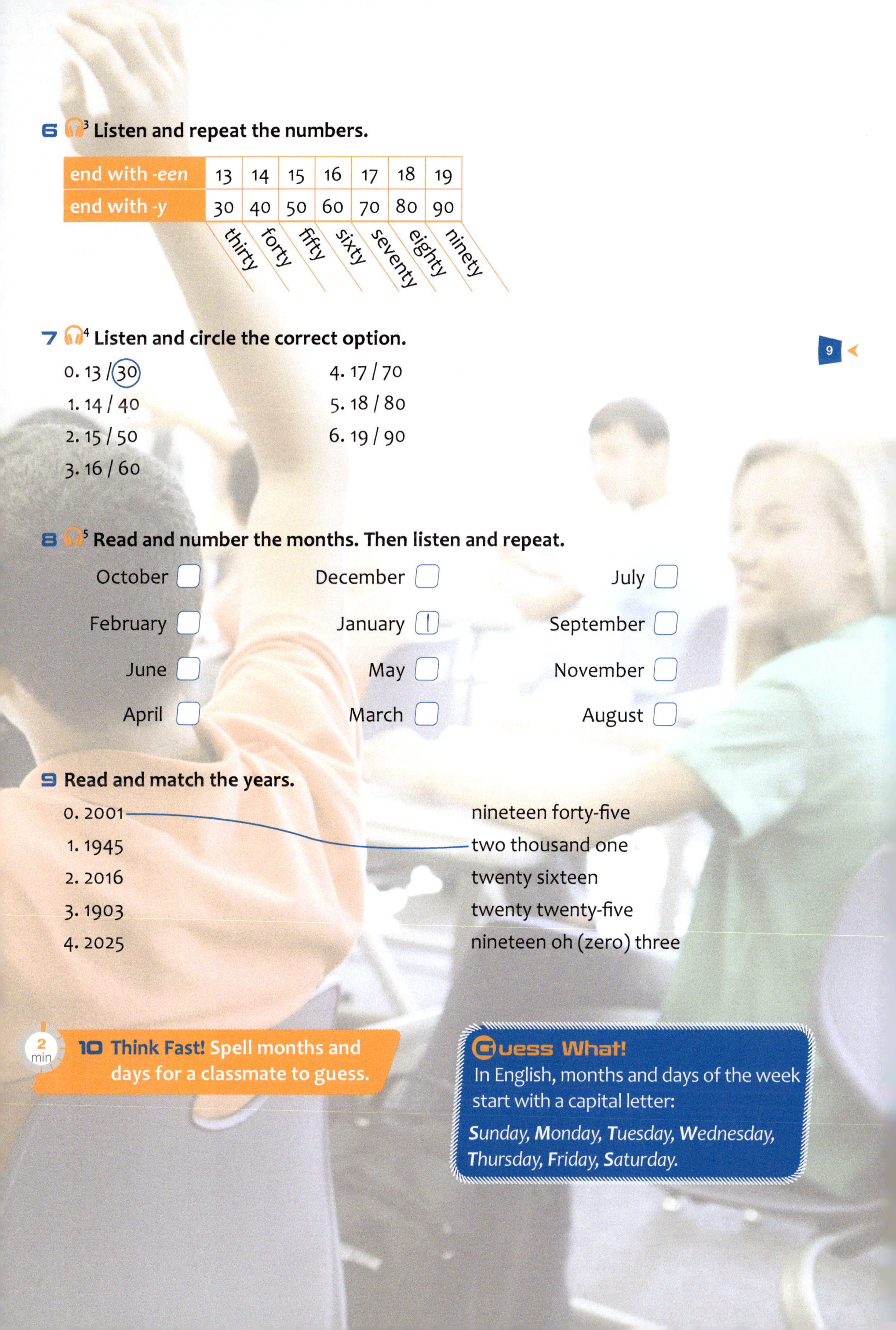

6 🎧3 **Listen and repeat the numbers.**

end with *-een*	13	14	15	16	17	18	19
end with *-y*	30	40	50	60	70	80	90
	thirty	forty	fifty	sixty	seventy	eighty	ninety

7 🎧4 **Listen and circle the correct option.**

0. 13 / (30)
1. 14 / 40
2. 15 / 50
3. 16 / 60
4. 17 / 70
5. 18 / 80
6. 19 / 90

8 🎧5 **Read and number the months. Then listen and repeat.**

October ☐ December ☐ July ☐

February ☐ January [1] September ☐

June ☐ May ☐ November ☐

April ☐ March ☐ August ☐

9 **Read and match the years.**

0. 2001 — two thousand one
1. 1945
2. 2016
3. 1903
4. 2025

nineteen forty-five
two thousand one
twenty sixteen
twenty twenty-five
nineteen oh (zero) three

2 min **10** **Think Fast! Spell months and days for a classmate to guess.**

Guess What!
In English, months and days of the week start with a capital letter:
***S**unday, **M**onday, **T**uesday, **W**ednesday, **T**hursday, **F**riday, **S**aturday.*

11 Listen and match the parts of the sentences.

Listen	to page 21.
Look	at the board.
Write	the correct option.
Circle	the text.
Read	to the conversation.
Open	your name.

Verbs and Nouns

Words that indicate actions are **verbs**. Words that represent people, places, things or ideas are **nouns**.

12 Look and circle the correct option.

0 

board / text

1 

page 21 / option

2 

name / conversation

13 Read and circle the words.

1. Circle nouns with blue.
2. Circle verbs with orange.

dictionary

English talk person

Paula Oliver listen

July write Monday

look computer read

Colors

- red
- orange
- yellow
- green
- blue
- purple
- black
- white
- brown
- gray

14 Look at the words and say the colors.

15 Read and complete the patterns.

0. Sunday, Tuesday, Thursday
1. ten, __________, twenty
2. nine, eleven, __________
3. December, November, __________
4. seven, __________, nine
5. thirty, sixty, __________

Subject Pronouns

	You
	She
	He
	It
	We
	They

Can

We use *can* to express ability. The form is the same for all subjects:
I can. / He can. / They can.

16 Look and write the correct subject pronoun.

0. (Sara) She
1. (Jason and Chris) ____________
2. (Owen) ____________
3. (Veronica) ____________
4. (Sara and I) ____________
5. (Sara and Veronica) ____________
6. () ____________

17 Classify the subject pronouns.

singular	________	you	________	________	________
plural	you	________	________		

18 Read and mark (✓) the sentences that are true for you.

1.  I can cook. ☐
2.  I can sing. ☐
3.  I can swim. ☐
4.  I can ride a bike. ☐
5.  I can dance. ☐
6.  I can skate. ☐
7.  I can play the guitar. ☐
8.  I can play basketball. ☐

1 min

19 Think Fast! Read and complete the sentences.

1. My favorite colors are ____________________ and ____________________.
2. My favorite day of the week is ____________________.
3. My favorite month is ____________________.

1

What is family?

Vocabulary

1 7 Listen and complete the family tree using the words in the box.

aunt brother cousin father grandfather
grandmother mother sister uncle

2 Read and identify the person.

1. Janice is my sister. Scott is my brother.
   Who am I? ____________________
2. Kirsty is my mother. Alexis is my aunt.
   Who am I? ____________________
3. Thomas is my uncle. Lee is my cousin.
   Who am I? ____________________
4. Alexis is my sister. Thomas is my brother.
   Who am I? ____________________

3 Imagine you are a member of this family.
Write clues for a classmate to guess the person.

1. ____

____

Who am I?

2. ____

____

Who am I?

4 Think Fast! Read a classmate's clues and guess the person.

1 min

5 Classify the family words in the chart.

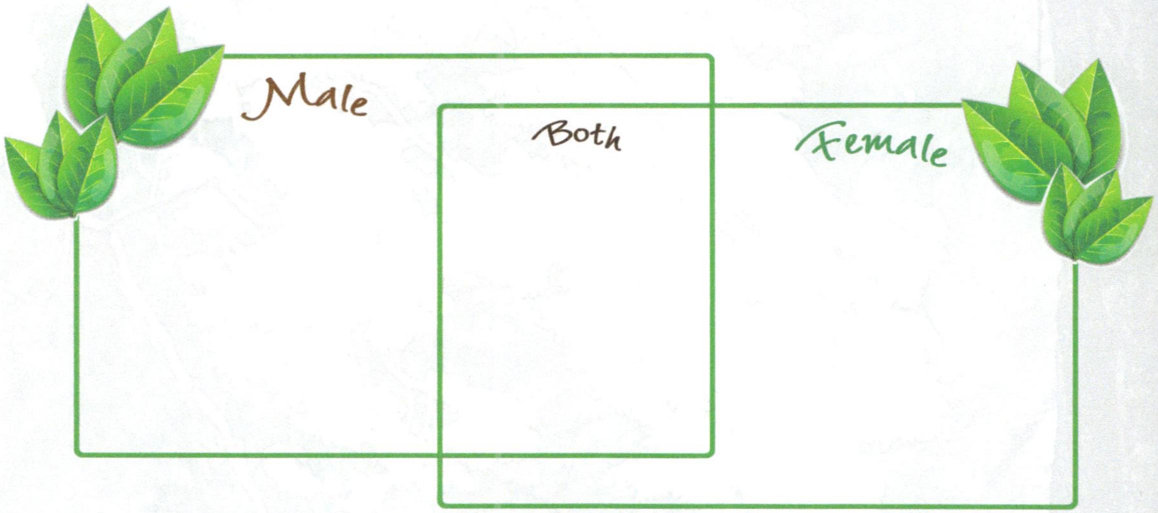

Guess What!

In everyday English, people say...

mother → **mom**
father → **dad**
(mom + dad = **parents**)

grandmother → **grandma**
grandfather → **grandpa**
(grandma + grandpa = **grandparents**)

Grammar

1 Look, read and complete the sentences.

_____________ are my grandparents.

_____________ is my cat.

_____________ are my cousins.

_____________ is my aunt.

_____________ is my house.

2 🎧8 Listen and repeat the words.

3 🎧9 Listen and memorize the rhyme.

This, that, **these** and those,
This is the way the T-H goes.
If you see your tongue pop out,
Then you have it all worked out!

Demonstratives

this singular + nearby	these plural + nearby
that singular + far	those plural + far

Possessive Adjectives

I	
you	your
he	
she	
it	its
we	our
they	

4 Underline the possessive adjectives and complete the chart.

1. My brother's name is Owen.
   He loves his baseball cap!

2. I have two sisters. Their names
   are Sara and Maggie.

3. My aunt's name is Veronica.
   Jason and Chris are her sons.

5 Read and complete using *is* or *are*.

1. This ____________ the Jo's family.
2. Sara and Maggie ____________ sisters.
3. Jason and Chris ____________ brothers.
4. Aunt Veronica ____________ their mother.

5 min

6 Think Fast! Look and write the sentences.

1. 

____

2.  / names / Paul and Shirley

____

3.  

____

4.  / name / Bill

____

Reading & Writing

1 Look at the pictures. What do you know about elephant families?

ELEPHANT FAMILIES

How much do you know about elephant families? African elephants live in groups called *herds*. A herd has elephant mothers, grandmothers, sisters, daughters, sons and cousins. Herds have around 12 members. The leader is a **female** elephant, the grandmother of the family. Elephant moms, aunts and sisters **take care of** the **calves**.

18

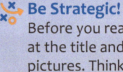

Be Strategic!
Before you read, look at the title and the pictures. Think about what you know.

Glossary

female: girl or woman

take care of: to give food to and protect

calves: (sing. calf) baby cows, elephants or whales

2 Read and circle *T* (True) or *F* (False).

1. A group of elephants is a herd. T F
2. Cousins are not in the herd. T F
3. The grandfather is the leader. T F
4. Elephants help each other. T F

3 Look and complete the sentences.

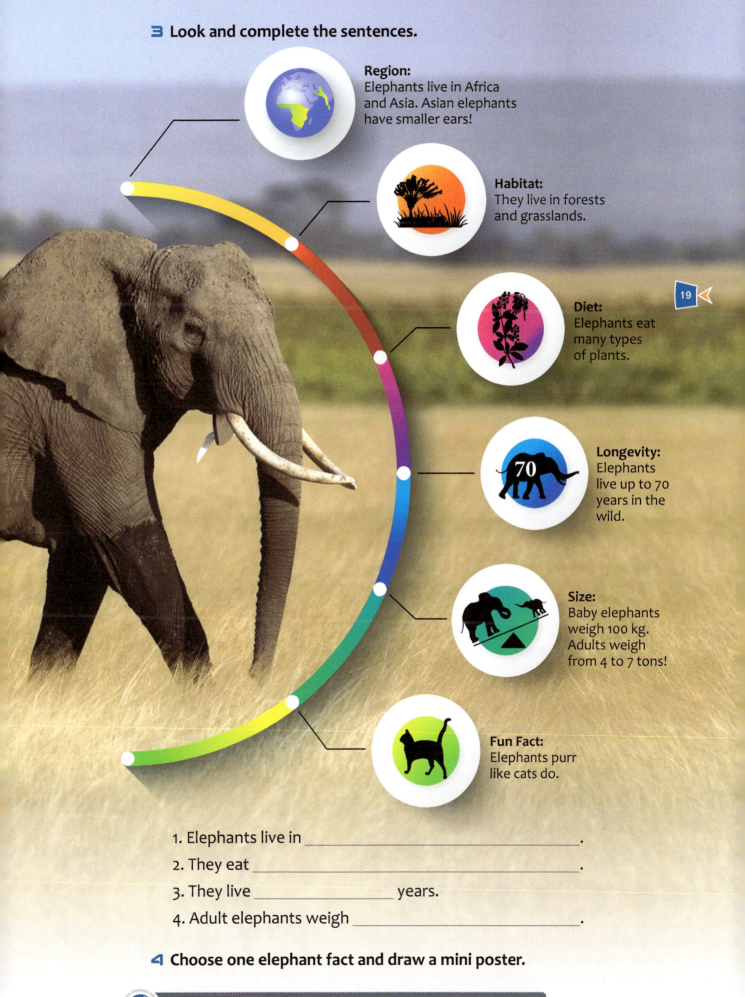

Region:
Elephants live in Africa and Asia. Asian elephants have smaller ears!

Habitat:
They live in forests and grasslands.

Diet:
Elephants eat many types of plants.

Longevity:
Elephants live up to 70 years in the wild.

Size:
Baby elephants weigh 100 kg. Adults weigh from 4 to 7 tons!

Fun Fact:
Elephants purr like cats do.

1. Elephants live in ______________________________.
2. They eat ______________________________.
3. They live ______________ years.
4. Adult elephants weigh ______________________________.

4 Choose one elephant fact and draw a mini poster.

Stop and Think! Is it OK to have circus elephants?

Culture

1 Read the sentences and circle the correct option.

1. Australia is in the northern / southern hemisphere.
2. It is near Greenland / New Zealand.
3. Native people in Australia are called Navajo / Aborigines.
4. Australia is famous for kangaroos and koalas / kiwis.
5. The capital city of Australia is Sydney / Canberra.

2 Read the comic and circle to complete the sentences.

1. The story takes place...
   a) on a hot day. b) on December 25. c) both a and b
2. Emily is from...
   a) Canada. b) Australia. c) the United States.
3. Emily is confused about some Australian...
   a) words. b) traditions. c) songs.
4. Emily learns to...
   a) ski. b) surf. c) swim.

3 **Write the Australian English words.**

1 

2 

3 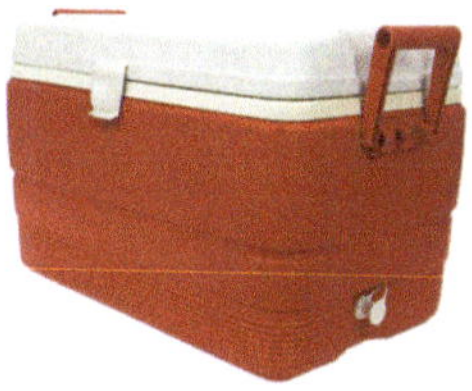

4 

5 

Stop and Think! What activities do you do with your family?

Glossary

g'day: hello
togs: swimsuit
barbie: barbeque
esky: a portable cooler
ace: great / very good!
tucker: food

Project

1 **Look at the Woods Family infographic on page 23. Write the headings from the infographic in the mind map.**

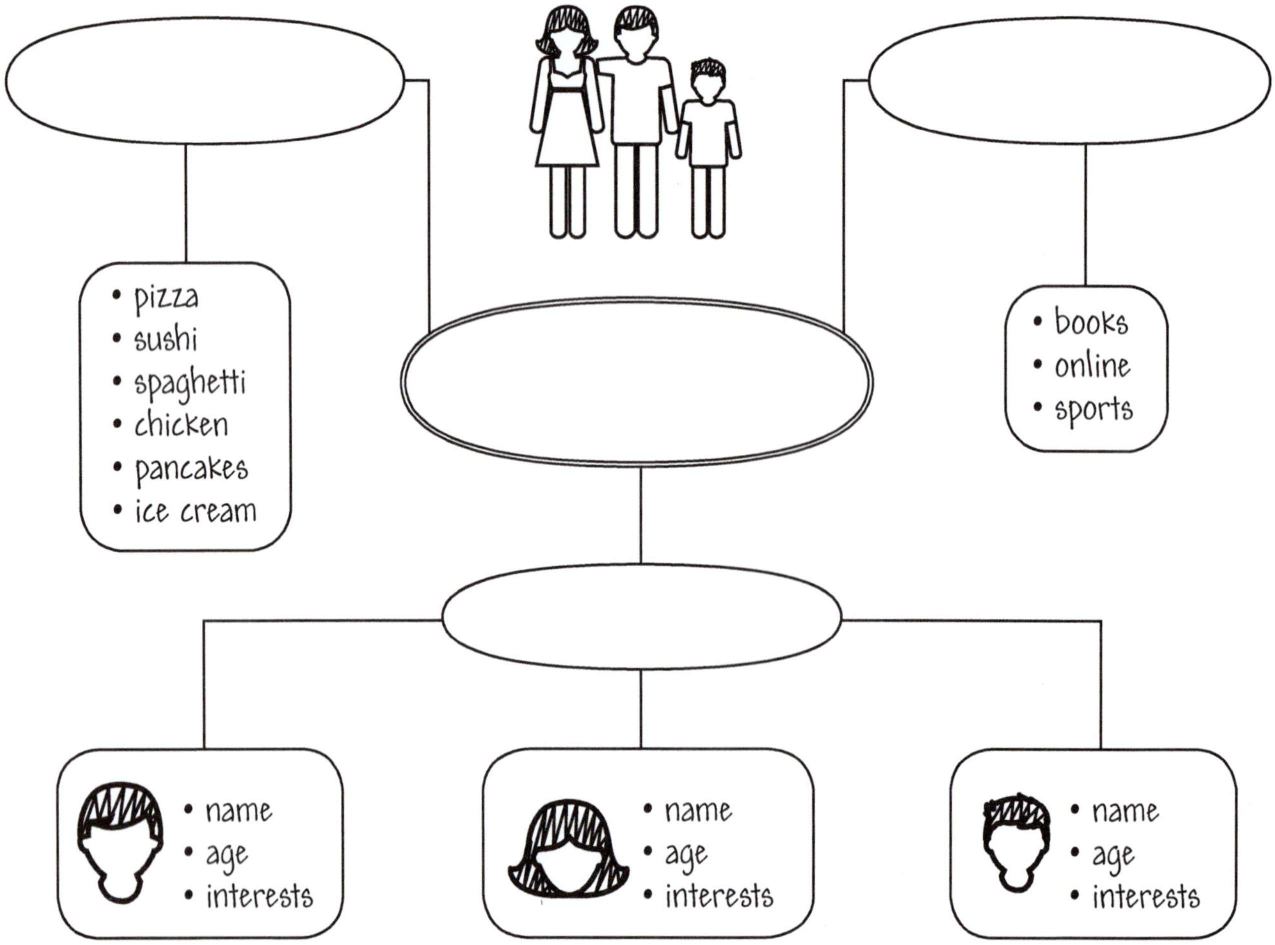

2 **In your notebook, make a mind map about your family.**

3 **Make a pie chart for your infographic.**

1. List your family's three favorite fun activities.
2. Estimate the number of hours your family does each activity in a week.

   6 hours reading books

   8 hours playing sports

   3 hours online
3. Add the numbers: 6 + 8 + 3 = 17. This is the total time for fun activities.
4. Divide the number of hours for each fun activity by the total time.

   6 hours reading books ÷ 17 (total hours) = 35%

   8 hours playing sports ÷ 17 = 47%

   3 hours online ÷ 17 = 18%
5. Use the percentages to make a fun activity pie chart.

4 **Make an infographic about your family. Present it to the class.**

The Woods Family

QUICK FACTS

DAD

name: Rick
age: 38
interests: model cars

MOM

name: Cathy
age: 37
interests: tennis

ME

name: Alex
age: 12
interests: swimming

FAVORITE FOODS

- pizza
- sushi
- spaghetti
- chicken
- pancakes
- ice cream

FUN ACTIVITIES

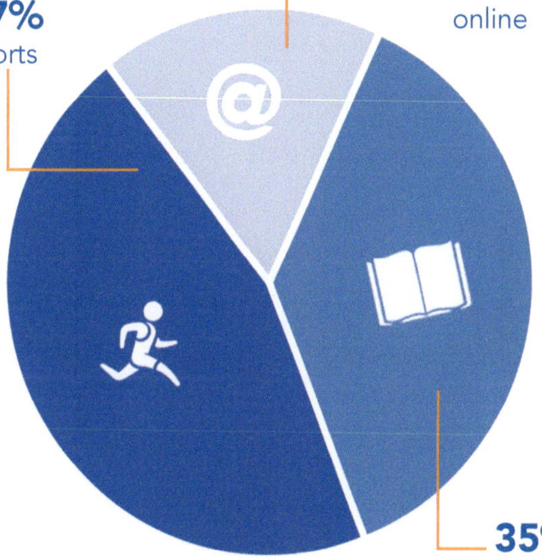

Review

1 Look and complete the sentences.

aunt
cousin
father
grandparents
mother
uncle

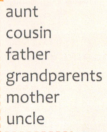

This is my family! Tom and Elizabeth are my (1) ________________. William is my (2) ________________. Anna is my (3) ________________ and Gavin is my (4) ________________. Michael is my (5) ________________. Daniela is my (6) ________________.

2 Read and circle *T* (True) or *F* (False).

1. Daniela is William's sister. T F
2. Anna is Gavin's aunt. T F
3. Michael is Lisa's brother. T F
4. Lisa is Gavin's niece. T F

3 Look and complete using *this*, *that*, *these* or *those*.

1. ________________ are my sisters.

2. ________________ is my cat.

3. ________________ are my parents.

4. ________________ is my neighbor.

5. ________________ are my cousins.

6. ________________ is my grandpa.

4 Follow and write the possessive adjectives.

1. I
2. you
3. she
4. he
5. it
6. we
7. they

5 Look and circle the correct option.

1. my / their dog

2. his / her garden

3. his / its sister

4. our / its food

6 Write questions using *is* and *are*.

1. Jackie / his / aunt

____

2. Ryan and Katie / your / cousins

____

3. that / his / sister

____

4. those / our / neighbors

____

5. Ellen / her / grandmother

____

6. these / my / parents

____

Just for Fun

1 Unscramble the words. Then decode the message.

TERMOH	☐☐☐☐☐☐	19, 8
TAFREH	☐☐☐☐☐☐	17, 18, 2
TERBRHO	☐☐☐☐☐☐☐	4
TISRES	☐☐☐☐☐☐	24, 22, 12
NOS	☐☐☐	14
DATHEGRU	☐☐☐☐☐☐☐☐	10, 5
CIOSUN	☐☐☐☐☐☐	15, 20, 11
TAUN	☐☐☐☐	1
LECNU	☐☐☐☐☐	21, 3
METNHARDORG	☐☐☐☐☐☐☐☐☐☐☐	6, 9, 13
TEDRAFNHRAG	☐☐☐☐☐☐☐☐☐☐☐	16, 23, 7

26

☐☐☐☐☐ ☐☐☐ ☐☐☐Y ☐YP☐☐ ☐☐ ☐☐☐☐☐☐☐☐ !

1 2 3 4 5   6 7 8   9 10 11   12 13 14   15 16   17 18 19 20 21 22 23 24

2 Read the clues and guess the person.

1. These are my (mother's daughter) ____________'s things.

2. These are my (father's brother) ____________'s things.

3. These are my (aunt's mother) ____________'s things.

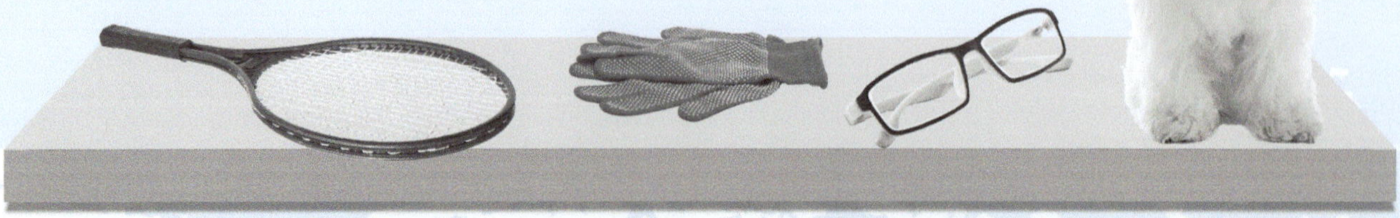

2

How do you learn?

Vocabulary

1 10 Listen and number the school places.

- [ ] art room
- [ ] auditorium
- [ ] bathrooms
- [ ] cafeteria
- [ ] classroom
- [ ] computer lab
- [ ] gymnasium
- [ ] laboratory
- [ ] library
- [ ] music room

2 Read and label the school subjects.

1. Ms. Satori teaches math in classroom 3B.
2. Mr. Thompson teaches chemistry in the laboratory.
3. Mr. Brooks teaches geography in classroom 1A.
4. Ms. Wilson teaches technology in the computer lab.
5. Coach Harris teaches P.E. in the gymnasium.
6. Ms. Taliafaro teaches physics in the auditorium.

3 11 Listen, clap and repeat.

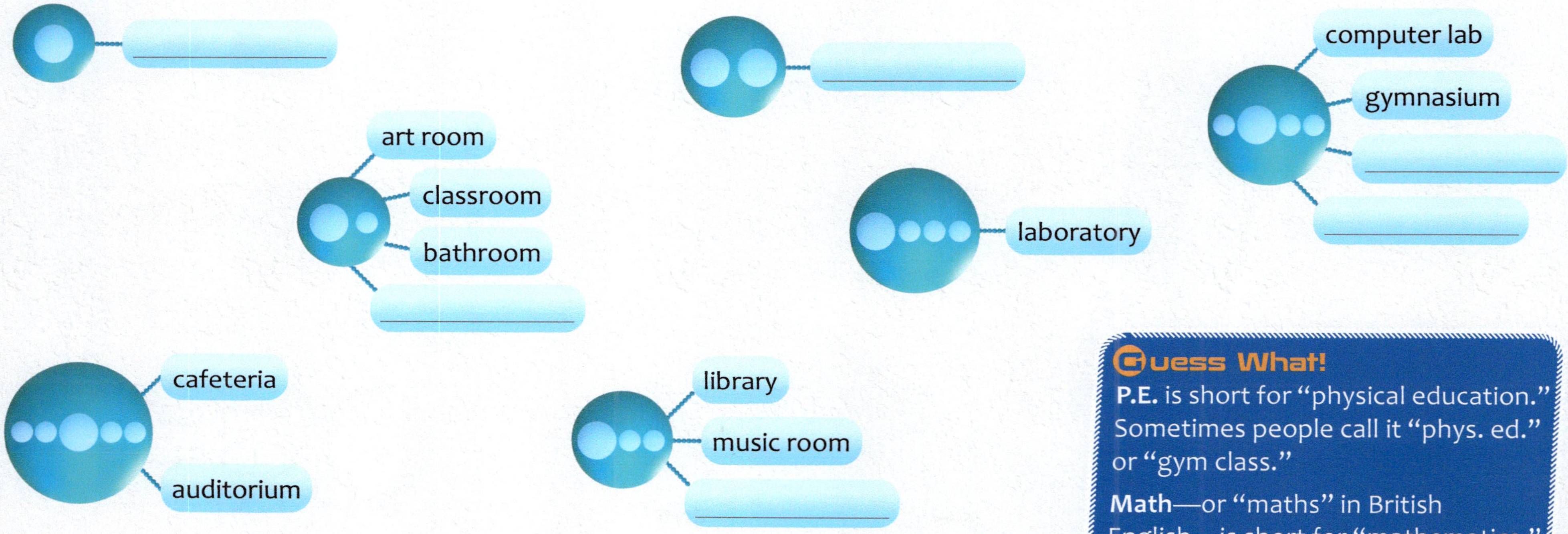

4 Think Fast! Add the school subjects to the chart.

5 min

Guess What!

P.E. is short for "physical education." Sometimes people call it "phys. ed." or "gym class."

Math—or "maths" in British English—is short for "mathematics."

Grammar

1 **Look and circle the correct option to complete the rules.**

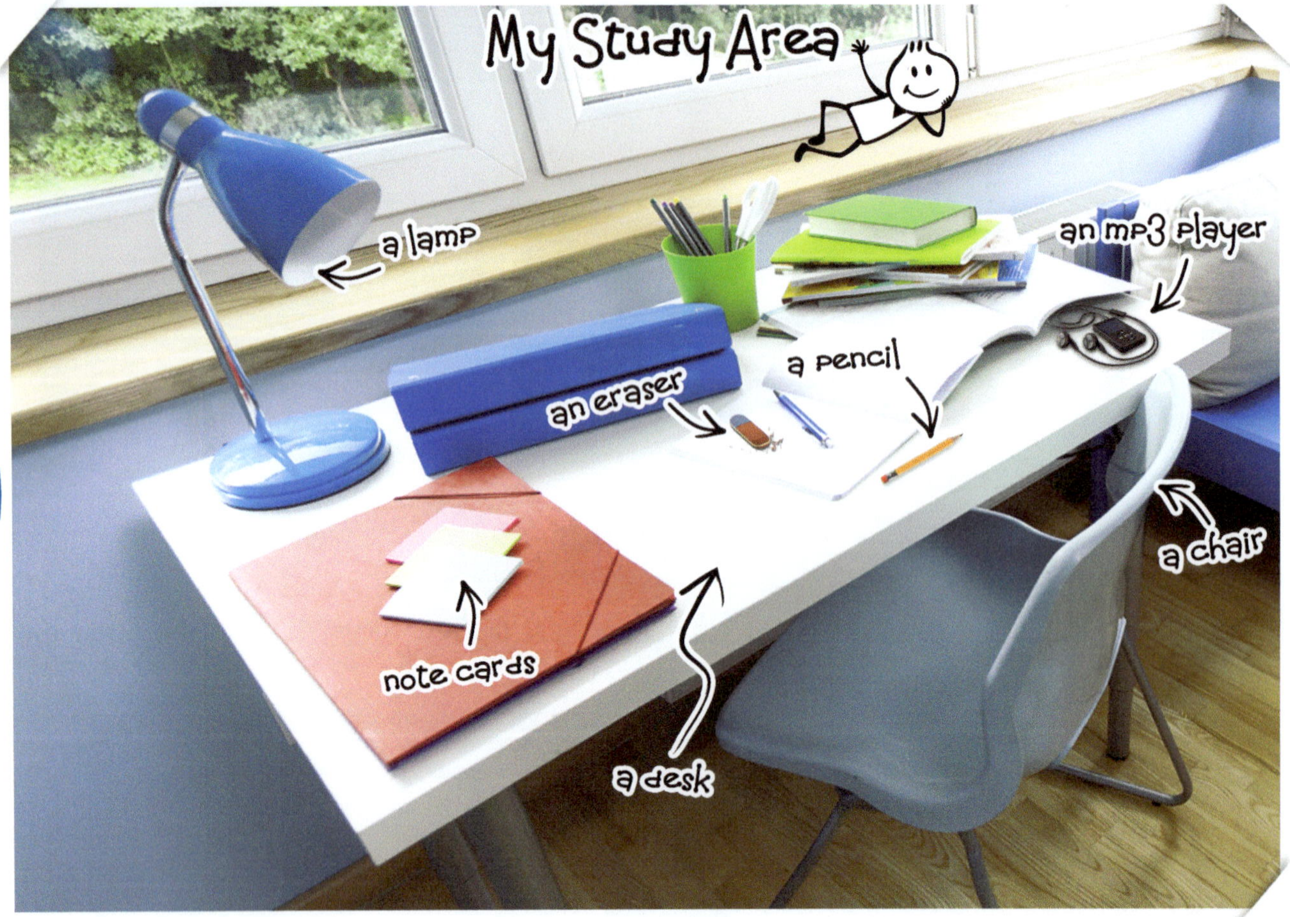

We use *a* or *an* before a noun to indicate a singular / plural object.

We use *a* before words that begin with a vowel / consonant sound.

We use *an* before words that begin with a vowel / consonant sound.

30

1 min **2** **Think Fast!** List five words that use *an*.

3 **Read and mark (✓) the correct picture.**

My brother has a lot of stuff in his backpack. He has a phone, some pens and a pencil. He also has a notebook and a calculator.

 ☐

 ☐

 ☐

Guess What!

Some words begin with a consonant letter but have a vowel sound: ***an*** *mp3 player*.
Some words begin with a vowel but have a consonant sound: ***a*** *university*.

4 Read and circle the correct answer.

1

Yes, I do. / No, I don't.

2

Yes, she does. / No, she doesn't.

3

Yes, they do. / No, they don't.

Verb *have*

he / she / it:
- \+ → has
- – → He doesn't have...
- ? → Does she have...?

I / you / we / they:
- \+ → have
- – → I don't have...
- ? → Do they have...?

Prepositions

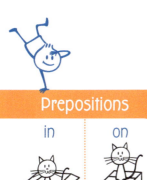

in	on

next to	under
	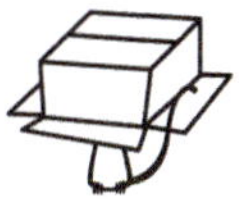

5 Look and complete the phrases.

1

_______________ the table

2

_______________ the backpack

3

_______________ the desk

4

_______________ the book

1 min

6 Think Fast! Write the questions in your notebook.

1. he / phone / his backpack?
2. they / notebooks / their desks?
3. you / calculator / your locker?
4. she / stapler / her desk?

Writing and Listening

1 Read the comic. Then write the school subjects to compare.

SCHOOL IN ANCIENT GREECE

MY SCHOOL

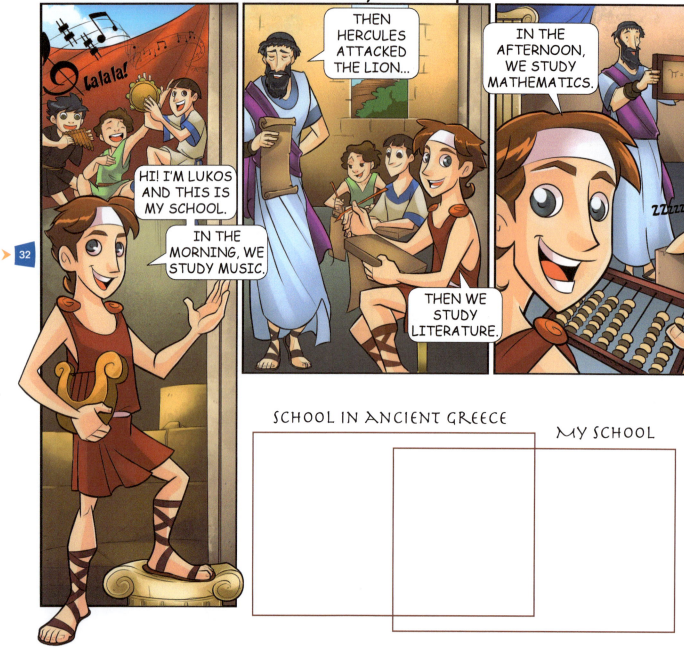

2 Look and label the subjects to complete the schedule.

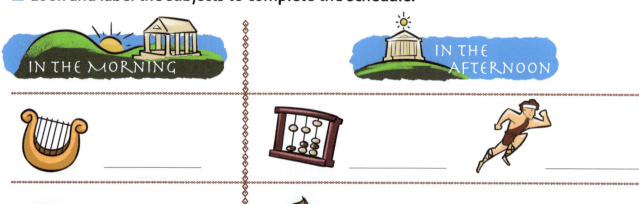

 ____________

 ____________

 ____________

 ____________

 ____________

Be Strategic! Before you listen, think about the topic and the words you will hear.

3 [12] **Listen and repeat the words.**

baking ☐

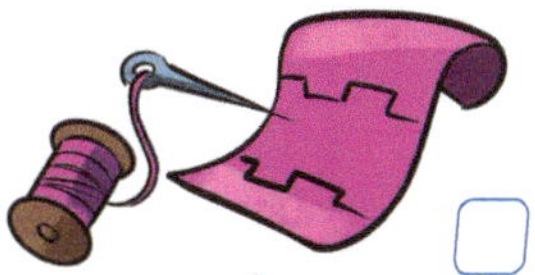
sewing ☐

dancing ☐

cooking ☐

childcare ☐

weaving ☐

4 [13] **Listen and number the subjects.**

5 **Design icons and make a schedule for your classes.**

Stop and Think! Should schools teach subjects like cooking, sewing and dancing? Should they teach childcare? Why? Why not?

Culture

1 Think Fast! Complete the table about your school day.

time at school	time studying	exercise	free time
hours	hours	hours	hours

2 Read and guess which sentences are true. Circle *T* (True) or *F* (False).

1. In China, many students live at their school. Guess: T F Answer: ________
2. Classes start at 8:00 a.m. Guess: T F Answer: ________
3. Students don't have a **break** for **lunch**. Guess: T F Answer: ________
4. Students **study** at **night**. Guess: T F Answer: ________
5. Students have many important exams. Guess: T F Answer: ________

3 14 **Listen and write *T* (True) or *F* (False).**

4 Read and complete the sentences.

Every morning, all students in China do radio gymnastics exercises. They listen to a radio program with music and they do exercises for ten minutes. This helps students to be alert for their studies. China also has special sports schools. Students go there to become professional **athletes**. It is very competitive.

1. All students do ______________________ exercises.
2. They listen to a ______________________ with music.
3. They do exercises for ______________________.
4. Students go to sports schools to become ______________________.
5. Sports school is very ______________________.

Stop and Think! What are the advantages and disadvantages of intense studying?

Glossary

break: a pause in activities

lunch: a meal in the middle of the day

study: to read and memorize information

night: after sunset

athletes: people who play sports well

Project

1 Look at the school collage on page 37. Mark (✓) the school features that you see.

1. Classrooms

desks

group tables

workshops

informal areas

2. Focus

business skills

interpersonal skills

artistic expression

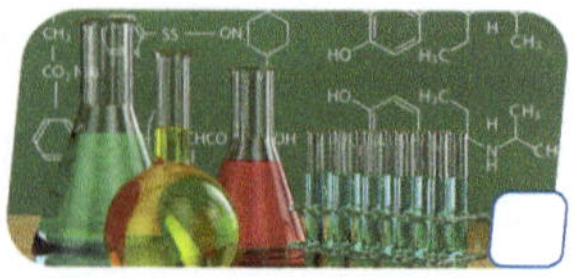
math and science

3. Sports

tennis

soccer

basketball

gymnastics

4. Extras

a pool

a robotics lab

delicious food

other ____________

2 15 Listen to the student explain his choices. Complete the sentences.

desks fun future practical really important would

This is my perfect school. It doesn't have regular ____________. It has group tables.
I ____________ like to have workshops for ____________ skills.
A math and science focus is ____________. It will help me in the ____________.
I think tennis is a good sport. It's ____________. I would like to have a pool.
I ____________ like swimming!

3 Choose one more school feature. Then make a collage.

Food

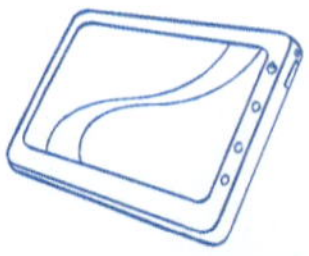
Technology

Clubs

Nature

4 In your notebook, write a description of your perfect school. Use the phrases in Activity 2.

The Perfect School

Classrooms

Focus

Extras

Sports

Review

1 Read the clues and write the school places.

1. glue, scissors, paints ________________
2. a basketball ________________
3. seats, a curtain, a podium ________________
4. encyclopedias, books ________________
5. trumpets, flutes, drums ________________
6. desks, a chalkboard ________________
7. tables, chairs, sandwiches ________________
8. a science experiment ________________

2 Correct the names of the school subjects.

1. fisical educacion ________________
2. geografy ________________
3. quemistry ________________
4. english ________________
5. cience ________________
6. tecnology ________________

3 Look and circle the correct option.

1 
a / an

2 

a / an

3 
a / an

4 
a / an

5 
a / an

6 

a / an

4 Complete the sentences using *have* or *has*.

1. Look! I ____________ a new backpack.
2. Katrina ____________ extra paper.
3. We ____________ two tests today!
4. The teacher ____________ my notebook.
5. Tyrone and Mason ____________ the stapler.

5 Unscramble the sentences.

1. has / Mike / tablet / his / locker / in / a

____

2. you / do / a / have / dictionary / ?

____

3. don't / my / a / have / parents / TV

____

4. does / Amanda / have / phone / a / ?

____

5. sister / have / a / my / calculator / doesn't

____

6 Read and complete using *Do* or *Does*.

1. ____________ you have art this morning?
2. ____________ Colin have an exam in the afternoon?
3. ____________ the band have practice after school?
4. ____________ our school have Wi-Fi?
5. ____________ you have a calculator?
6. ____________ Amy have a sister?

7 Find the missing objects. Then write four sentences.

backpack calculator jacket pencil

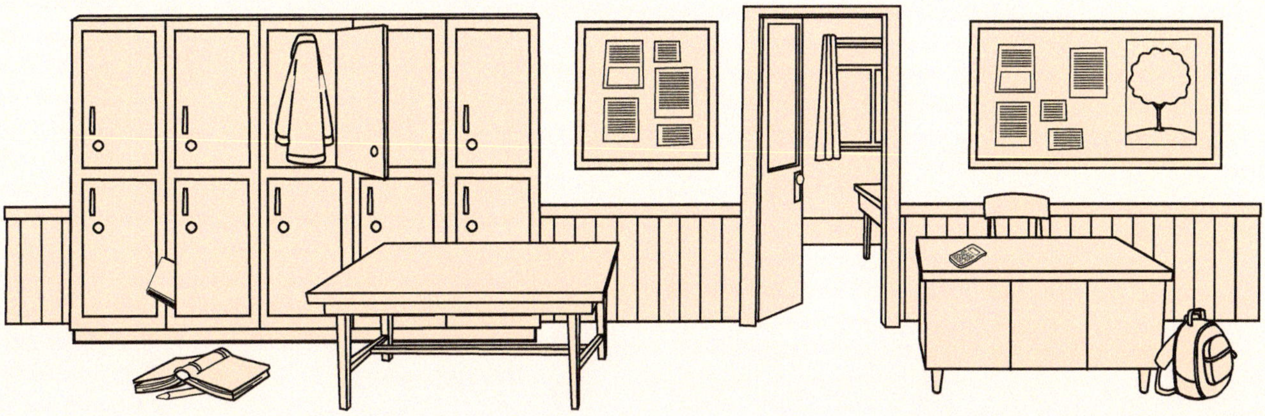

1. (under) ____
2. (in) ____
3. (next to) ____
4. (on) ____

2 min **8 Think Fast!** Describe the locations of five objects in your classroom.

Just for Fun

1 **Look and write the school places.**

1

2

3

4

5

6

2 **Read and solve the puzzle with school subjects.**

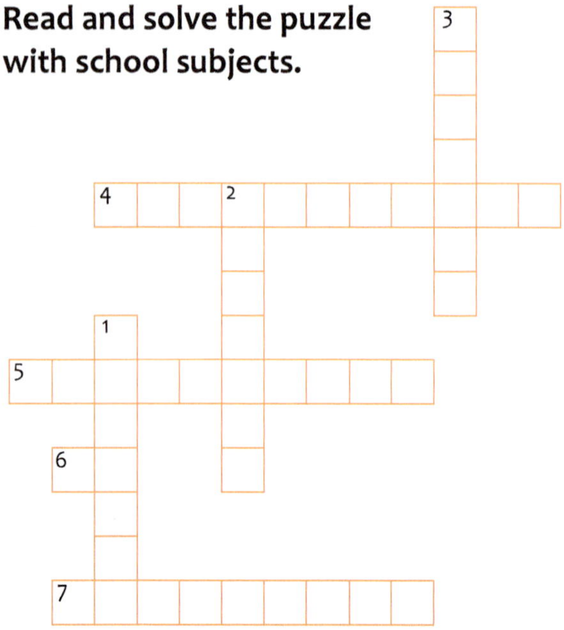

Down
1. physics, chemistry and biology
2. past events
3. food preparation

Across
4. calculations
5. tablets and computers
6. physical education
7. regions and countries

3

Where are you from?

Vocabulary

1 [16] Listen and number the landmarks.

The Sydney Opera House ☐

The Great Wall of China ☐

Tower Bridge ☐

Machu Picchu ☐

The Taj Mahal ☐

Central Park ☐

The Great Pyramid ☐

Christ the Redeemer ☐

1 Australia

2 Brazil

3 China

4 Egypt

5 India

6 Peru

7 The United Kingdom

8 The United States

2 Listen and write the nationality for each country. [17]

1. ______________________
2. ______________________
3. ______________________
4. ______________________
5. ______________________
6. ______________________
7. ______________________
8. ______________________

Guess What!
It is common to say "The UK" for the United Kingdom and "The US" for the United States.

3 Read and match.

1. French
2. Turkish
3. Italian
4. Thai
5. Greek
6. Japanese

 Japan

 Greece

 France

 Italy

 Thailand

 Turkey

4 Classify the nationality words.

Country + *-ian* or *-n*	
Country + *-ish*	
Country + *-ese*	
Other	

5 min

5 Think Fast! In your notebook, write eight nationality words in alphabetical order.

Grammar

1 Read and label the information cards.

ENDANGERED SPECIES

Diet:	They are **carnivores.**
Region:	They live in eastern Russia.
Ability:	They can **swim.**
Interesting fact:	They're the biggest cats in the world.

Diet:	They are carnivores.
Region:	Northern Russia and North America.
Ability:	They can swim.
Interesting fact:	Their **fur** isn't white. It's **clear**!

Diet:	They are **herbivores.**
Region:	They live in the mountains of central China.
Ability:	They can climb trees.
Interesting fact:	They eat 20 kg of bamboo every day!

Diet:	They are carnivores.
Region:	They live in the world's oceans.
Ability:	They can jump.
Interesting fact:	They aren't white. They're gray!

Diet:	They are **omnivores.**
Region:	They live on the **islands** of Borneo and Sumatra.
Ability:	They can learn **sign language.**
Interesting fact:	Their name means "person of the forest."

Glossary

carnivores: animals that eat other animals
swim: to move in water
fur: animal hair
clear: transparent
herbivores: animals that eat only plants
omnivores: animals that eat plants and animals
islands: land surrounded by water
sign language: a language of gestures for people who can't speak or hear

Siberian Tigers

Orangutans

Giant Pandas

Polar Bears

Great White Sharks

2 Underline the forms of *be* in the information cards.

be	+	–
I	am ('m)	am not ('m not)
he / she / it	is ('s)	is not (isn't)
you / we / they	are ('re)	are not (aren't)

1 min

3 Think Fast! Look and write the contraction.

1. are not ______
2. they are ______
3. it is ______
4. is not ______
5. are not ______
6. I am ______
7. you are ______
8. she is ______
9. he is ______
10. we are ______

4 Complete the information card with the correct form of *be*.

Galapagos Tortoises

Type: They ______ reptiles.
Diet: They ______ herbivores.
Region: They live in the Galapagos Islands.
Ability: They can live 150 years!
Interesting fact: They'______ very heavy! They weigh 250 kg.

Guess What!
People use contractions in most situations.
People don't use contractions in formal texts.

Reading and Speaking

1 [18] **Listen and circle the correct option.**

1. Fusun is American / Turkish.
2. She's from Istanbul / Ankara.
3. Istanbul is / isn't the capital of Turkey.

Be Strategic!
Read in steps: First, read quickly to get a general idea of the topic. Then read carefully to understand the details.

2 Look, read and number.

Places to See in Istanbul!

In the Egyptian Spice **Bazaar**, you can **try** Turkish delight, a traditional **candy**. You can also try some Turkish coffee. ☐

You can go shopping at the Grand Bazaar. Buy **souvenirs** and eat kebab, a popular Turkish food. ☐

Many people visit the Hagia Sophia to see its incredible architecture. ☐

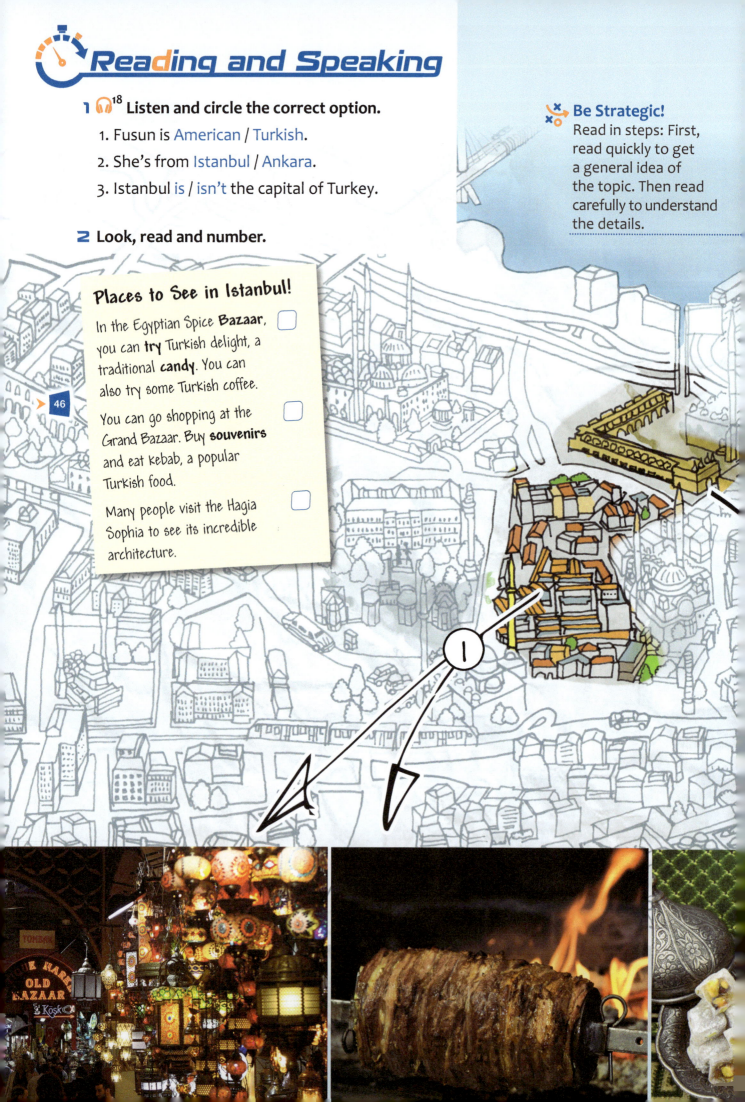

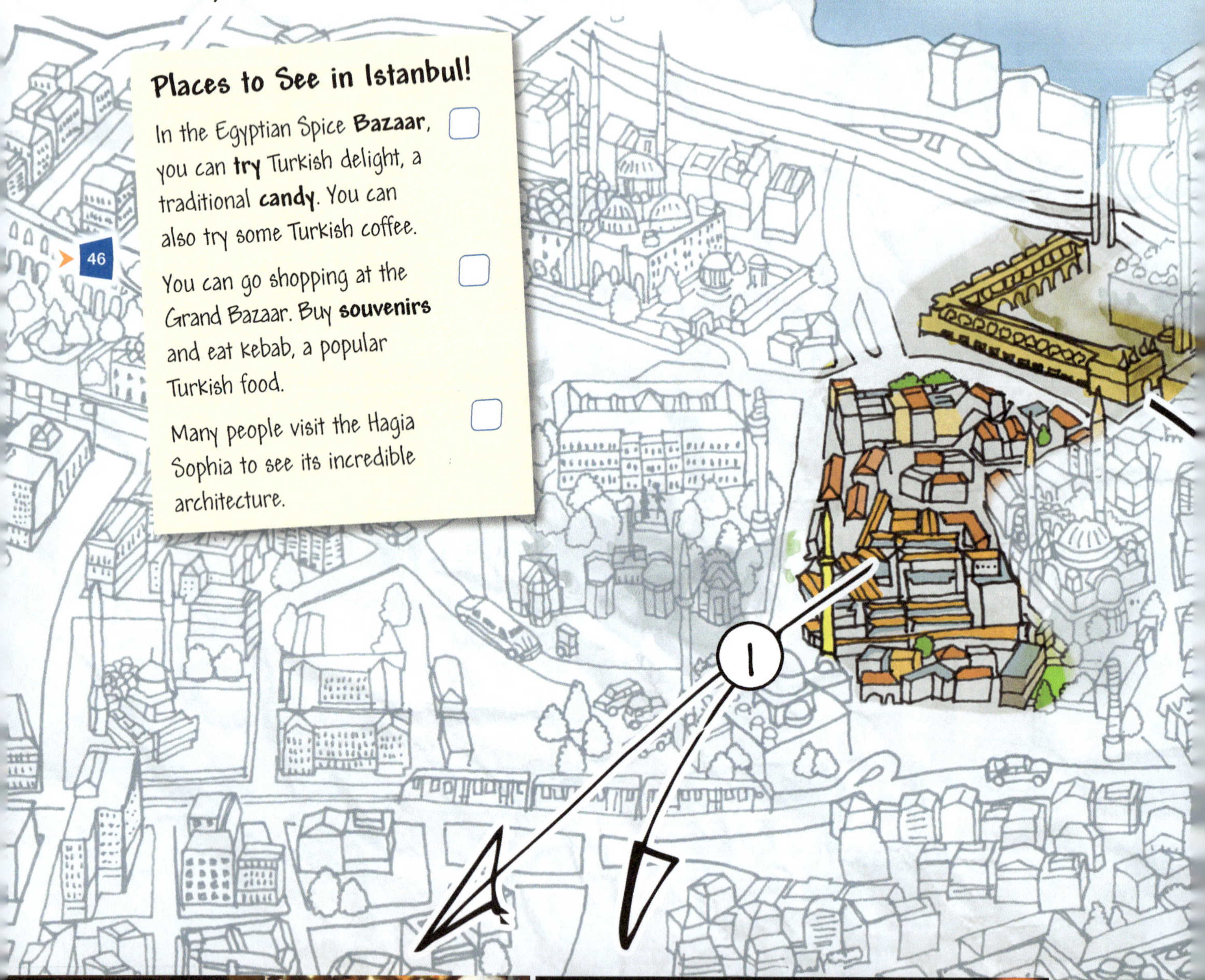

3 **Complete the table about a city you know.**

City or Town ______________________________

Landmarks	Shopping	Local Foods

4 **Present the city or town.**

Stop and Think!
What is special about your city or town?

Glossary

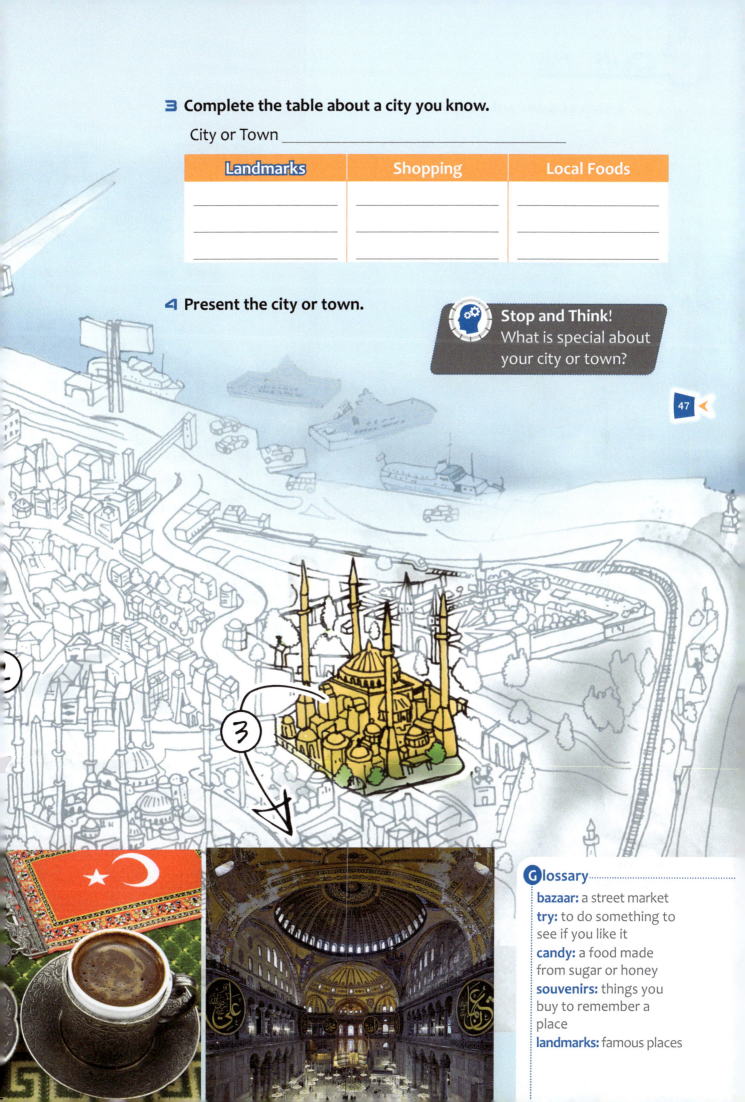

bazaar: a street market
try: to do something to see if you like it
candy: a food made from sugar or honey
souvenirs: things you buy to remember a place
landmarks: famous places

Culture

1 19 **Listen and write the captions.**

The Festival of Holi
Bollywood Movies
Henna
Transportation

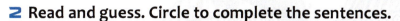

2 **Read and guess. Circle to complete the sentences.**

What do you know about India?

1. India is a country...
   a) in Southeast Asia.   b) in Northern Africa.   c) in Antarctica.
2. India has 780...
   a) languages.   b) cities.   c) universities.
3. The official languages are...
   a) Hindi and Arabic.   b) Hindi and English.   c) Hindi and Telugu.
4. The capital city of India is...
   a) Mumbai.   b) Kolkata.   c) New Delhi.
5. The population of India is...
   a) 1.2 million.   b) 120 million.   c) 1.2 billion.

Answers: 1. a 2. a 3. b 4. c 5. c

3 20 **Listen and number the Indian instruments.**

4 **Read the recipe. What is it similar to?**

Mango Lassi

Ingredients

- 1 cup of **plain** yogurt
- ½ cup of milk
- 1 mango
- 4 teaspoons of sugar

Glossary

paint: a substance that adds color
designs: patterns with shapes or lines
plain: simple

Stop and Think! What do you like about your country?

Project

1 Look at the country profile and complete the sentences.

The South African flag has six colors:

________, ________,

________, ________,

________ and ________.

CAPITAL CITY

The capital of South Africa is ________.

POPULATION

The population is ________.

LANGUAGES

South Africa has ________ official languages!

LANDMARKS

You can visit ________ Mountain and ________ National Park.

TRADITIONAL FOODS

You can try ________ and ________.

POPULAR SPORTS

The most popular sports are ________, ________ and ________.

WILDLIFE

You can see ________, ________, ________, ________, ________, ________ and ________.

2 Choose a country and make a country profile.

SOUTH AFRICA

Official Languages:
English, Afrikaans, Zulu, Xhosa, Southern Sotho, Tswana, Northern Sotho, Venda, Tsonga, Swati, Ndebele

Population:
53 million

A white rhinoceros in Kruger National Park

Braaivleis

Popular Sports:
cricket, rugby, soccer

Wildlife:
elephants
leopards
lions
rhinoceroses
buffaloes
giraffes
penguins
... and many more!

Traditional Foods:
bobotie (ground meat, eggs and spices)
braaivleis (barbecued meat)

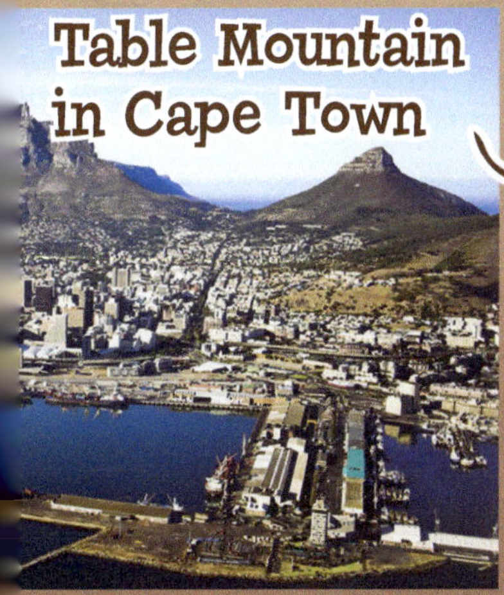
Table Mountain in Cape Town

Bobotie

Review

1 Look and complete the country names. Then write the nationalities.

1. U__________d K__________m

I'm __________!

2. P__________

I'm __________!

3. In__________

I'm __________!

4. Au__________

I'm __________!

5. U__________d S__________s

I'm __________!

6. E__________

I'm __________!

7. Ch__________

I'm __________!

8. Br__________

I'm __________!

2 Classify the words.

France   Greek   Italy   Japanese   Thai   Turkey

Country	Nationality

3 Look and write the sentences.

1. The capital of India / Mumbai ✗

____

2. Tokyo / the capital of Japan ✓

____

3. Rome and Venice / Italian cities ✓

____

4. Cairo / the capital of Peru ✗

____

5. New York and Boston / in the United States ✓

____

4 Read and complete the information card.

The American Crocodile

Diet: Crocodiles __________ carnivores.

Region: They live in North and South America.

Ability: They _______ swim 32 km per hour.

They _______ run, too!

Interesting fact:

Crocodiles __________ live up to 60 years.

The Bottlenose Dolphin

5 Look and write the contractions.

1. Dolphins live in the ocean, but they are not fish. __________
2. They are very intelligent. __________
3. The bottlenose dolphin is not very big. __________
4. It is usually three meters long. __________
5. Dolphins can not smell odors. __________

Just for Fun

1 Look and number the countries.

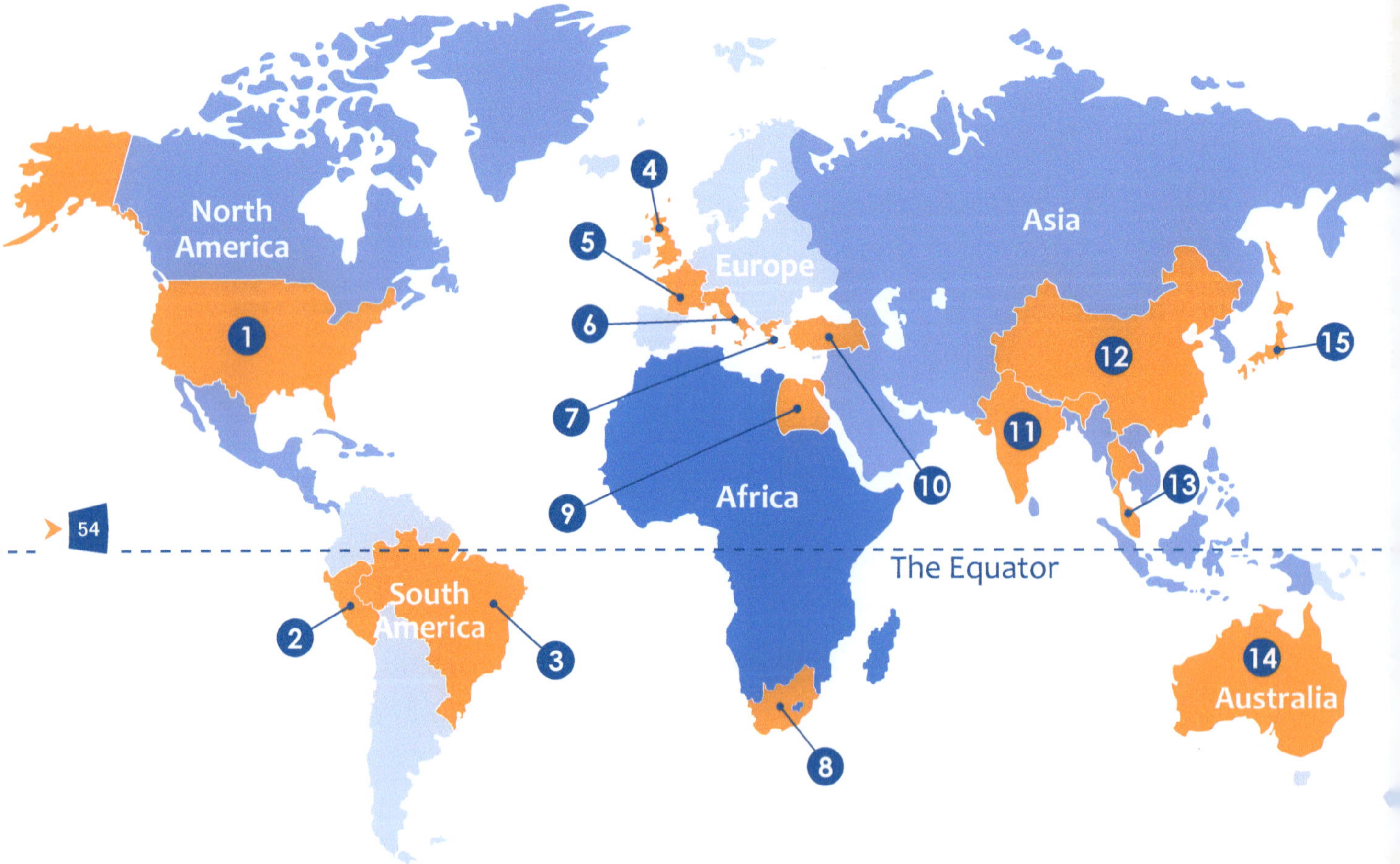

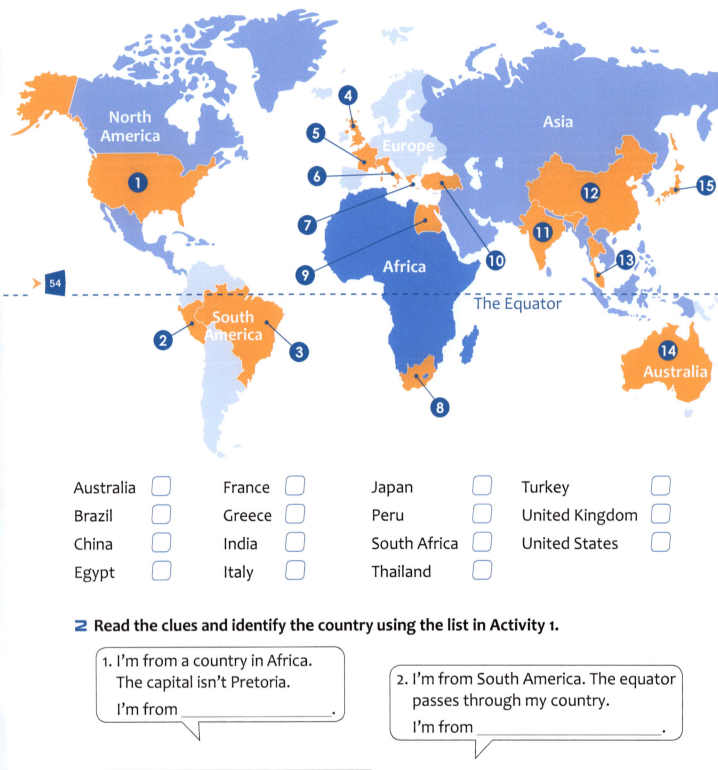

Australia	☐	France	☐	Japan	☐	Turkey	☐
Brazil	☐	Greece	☐	Peru	☐	United Kingdom	☐
China	☐	India	☐	South Africa	☐	United States	☐
Egypt	☐	Italy	☐	Thailand	☐		

2 Read the clues and identify the country using the list in Activity 1.

1. I'm from a country in Africa. The capital isn't Pretoria.
   I'm from ______________________.

2. I'm from South America. The equator passes through my country.
   I'm from ______________________.

3. I'm from Europe, but I'm not French or Italian. The capital of my country isn't London.
   I'm from ______________________.

4. I'm from a country in Asia. I'm not Chinese, Indian or Japanese. The capital of my country isn't Ankara.
   I'm from ______________________.

4

What is home?

Vocabulary

1 21 **Listen and complete.**

Appliances

 r_fr___rat_r

 st__e

 t___v__ion

 __sh__

 dr___

Furniture

 t_bl_

 __d

 s__a

 ch___

Fixtures

 _in_

 sh_w__

 t__l_t

Guess What!
There are short forms for many English words:
refrigerator → **fridge**
television → **TV**

2 Read and number the rooms.

1. The kitchen has a refrigerator and a stove.
2. The living room has a sofa and a television.
3. The bathroom has a sink, a toilet and a shower.
4. The dining room has a table and chairs.
5. The bedroom has a bed.
6. The laundry room has a washer and dryer.

3 22 **Listen and write the room.**

1. ______________________
2. ______________________
3. ______________________
4. ______________________
5. ______________________
6. ______________________

4 Look and match.

1. washer 2. refrigerator 3. shower 4. sink 5. bed

30 sec

5 Think Fast! Look and identify the room.

1 
2 
3 
4 

5 
6 
7 
8 

Grammar

1 Read and number the objects in the pictures.

1. There are old photos on the wall in the living room.
2. There's a mirror in the bathroom.
3. There's a red chair between the lamp and the TV.
4. There's a table in the kitchen. It's next to the window.
5. There are lots of magnets on the fridge.
6. There are two lamps in the bedroom.
7. There's a green chair in front of the window.

There is / are

✓ There is...
✓ There are...
✗ There isn't..
✗ There aren't (any)...

At My Grandma's Apartment!

Guess What!
In British English, people say "flat" not apartment. They also, informally, call a bathroom a "loo."

2 Read and complete the description.

isn't   is   are   is   isn't   aren't

This is my grandma's apartment. It (1) __________ very big, but it (2) __________ very comfortable. There (3) __________ four rooms: a kitchen, a living room, a bedroom and a bathroom. There (4) __________ an old TV in the living room. There (5) __________ a washer and there (6) __________ any plants.

3 Circle the correct option. Then complete the answers.

1. Is / Are there a dining room? No, there isn't.
2. Is / Are there a bathroom? Yes, ______________ is.
3. Is / Are there a cat? Yes, ______________.
4. Is / Are there a dog? No, ______________.
5. Is / Are there chairs? Yes, ______________.
6. Is / Are there plants? No, there ______________.

4 Read and match.

1. Where's the green chair?	They're on the fridge.
2. Where are the magnets?	It's in front of the window.
3. Where's the cat?	They're on the wall.
4. Where are the photos?	It's on the bed.

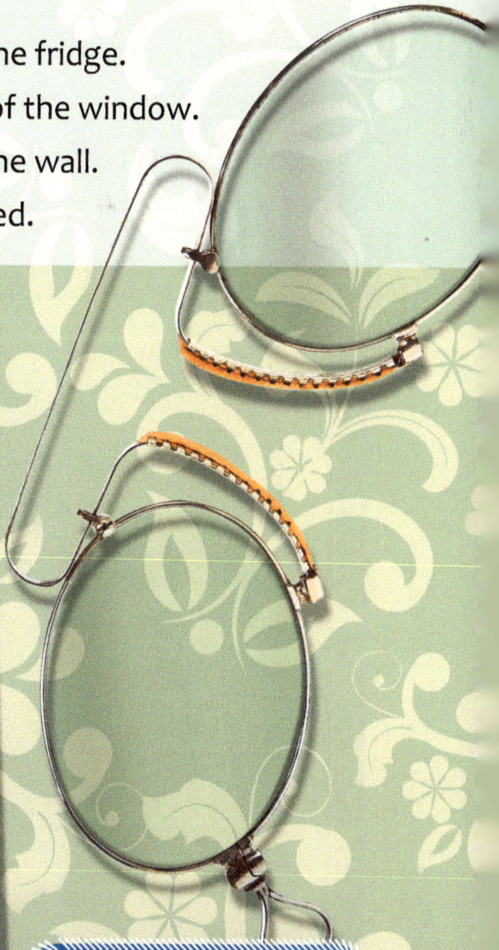

3 min

5 Think Fast! In your notebook, write ten sentences to describe your house.

Guess What!
We use *Where* to ask about the location of people or things.

Listening and Reading

1 23 Listen and write *D* (Debbie), *A* (Aaron) or *M* (Miles).

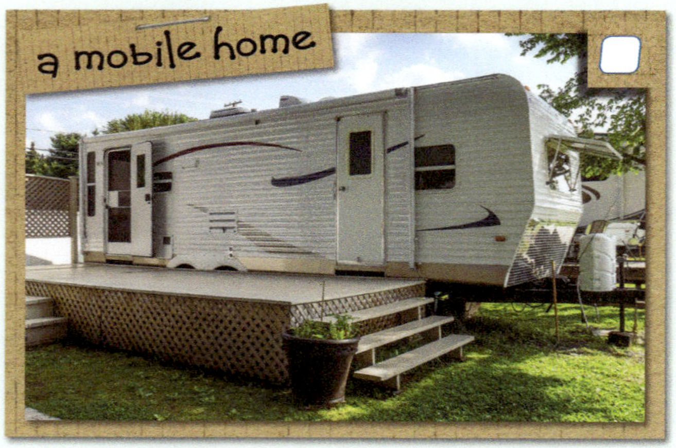

Be Strategic!
Look carefully at the photos and make predictions about what you will hear: Where is the home? Is it big or small?

2 23 **Listen again and identify the person.**

Home is just a place to sleep. ______

Home is a place to **relax.** ______

Home is about family. ______

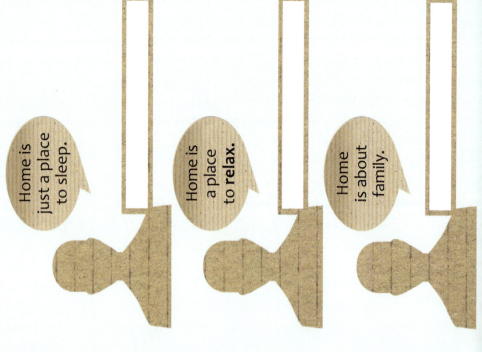

3 **Read and guess the answers. Then compare with a classmate.**

In the United States...

of houses have a garage.

of homeowners have children.

of houses have a dining room.

of homeowners have pets.

of houses have two or more bathrooms.

4 24 **Listen and and check.**

Stop and Think! What makes a place into a home?

Glossary

farm: land for producing food

lake: a large area of water

relax: to rest or enjoy leisure activities

work: to do a job

enough: sufficient

United States Census Bureau. (May 2015). 2013 *Housing Profile: The United States. American Housing Survey Factsheets.*

Culture

1 Look and circle the correct option.

1. These people are from northern Africa / Asia .
2. This area is mostly desert / mountains .
3. People live in bungalows / tents .
4. They use camels / horses for transportation.
5. The climate is very cold / hot .

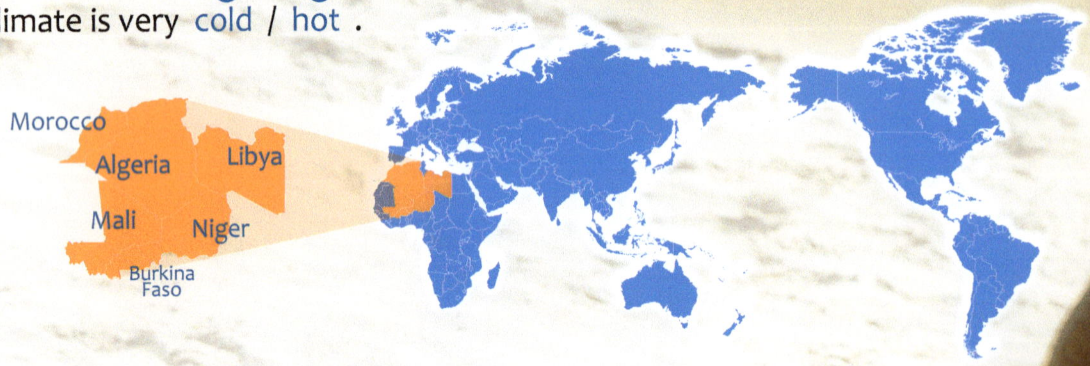

2 Read the text and complete the sentences.

The Tuareg people live in the Sahara Desert in Northern Africa. They live in six different countries: Algeria, Morocco, Libya, Mali, Niger and Burkina Faso. There are about two **million** Tuareg and they are **nomads**. The traditional Tuareg home is a tent made from camel hair. They don't have a lot of furniture. Tuareg men wear **turbans**. They **cover** their faces as a part of their religion. Tuareg women and children don't cover their faces.

1. The Tuareg live in the ______________________ Desert.
2. They live in a region that includes ______________________ different countries.
3. There are about two ______________________ Tuareg in Northern Africa.
4. Their tents are made from ______________________ hair.
5. Tuareg men wear ______________________.

Survival in the Desert

3 25 **Listen and number the photos.**

☐ turbans

☐ an oasis

☐ camels

☐ the stars

☐ mint tea

Guess What!
The Tuareg people have mixed racial characteristics. Some have very dark skin and some do not. Some have blue eyes!

Stop and Think! What are the advantages and disadvantages of the Tuareg way of life? What can we learn from them?

Glossary

million: 1,000,000
nomads: people who don't live in a fixed location
turbans: cloth wrapped around the head
cover: to put cloth over something in order to protect it
survive: to live in difficult conditions
oasis: a place with water and plants in the desert

Project

1 Look at page 65 and mark (✓) the features of the home design.

Type of Home

a cabin

an apartment

a mansion

a houseboat

Location

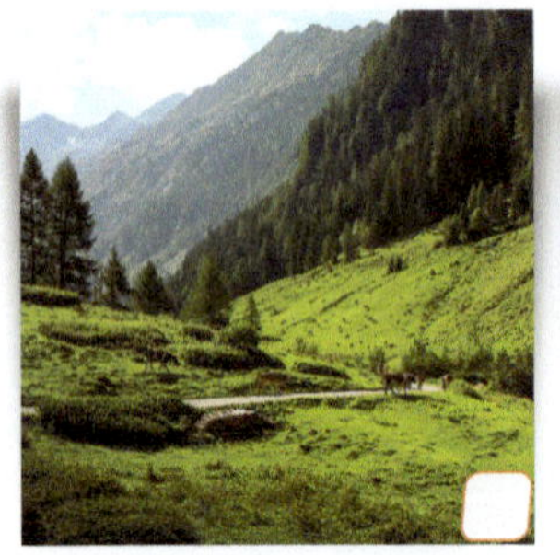
in the mountains

by the sea

in the city

in the countryside

Style

modern

rustic

formal

casual

Decorations

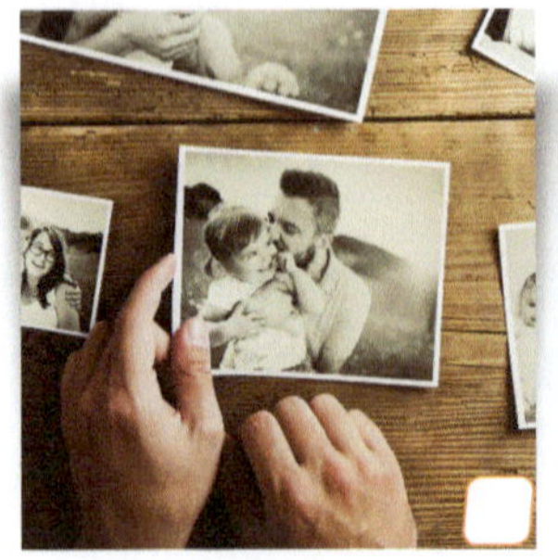
photos

plants

paintings

flowers

2 Design a home using the characteristics in Activity 1. Describe the furniture, fixtures and appliances.

3 Present your design to the class.

My home

My home is a houseboat in the city. The style is casual. It has plants and flowers.

Living Room

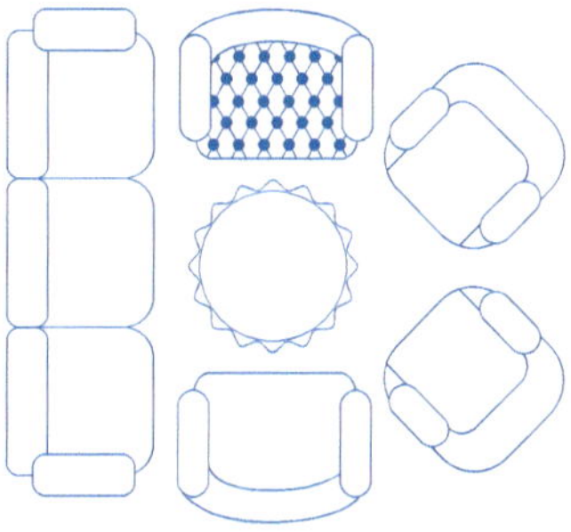

There are four chairs. There is a sofa and a table.

Bedroom

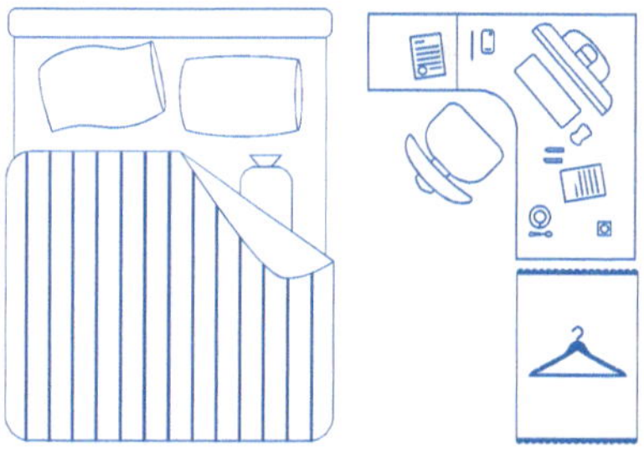

There is a bed, a desk and a closet.

Kitchen

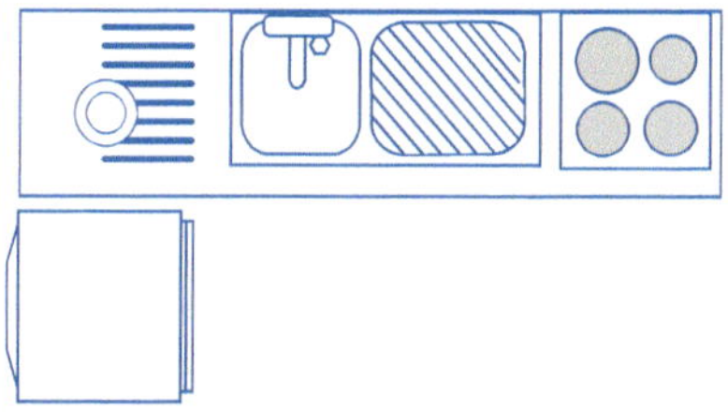

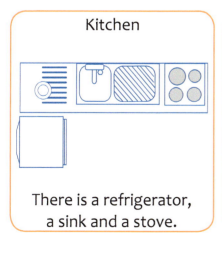

There is a refrigerator, a sink and a stove.

Dining Room

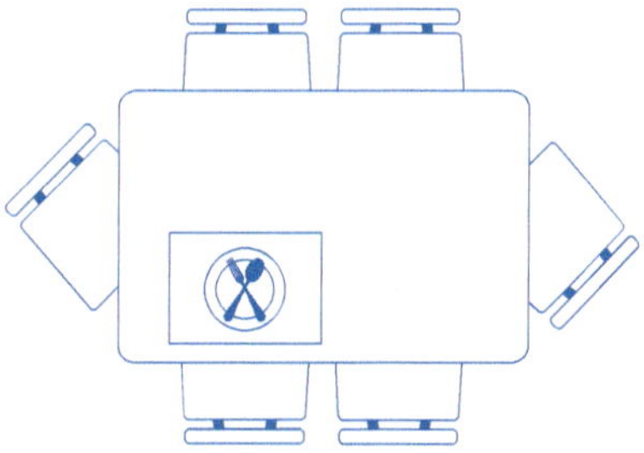

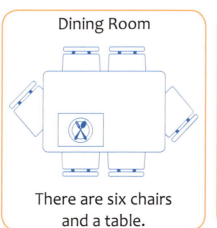

There are six chairs and a table.

Bathroom

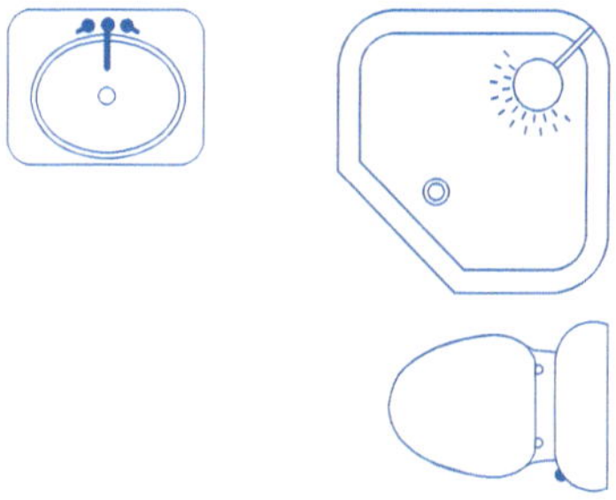

There is a sink, a shower and a toilet.

Review

1 Look and label the rooms.

1 

2 

3 

4 

5 

6 

2 Look and circle the correct option.

1 
stove / lamp

2 
toilet / sink

3 
shower / washer

4 
bed / table

5 
sofa / chair

3 Look, read and mark (✓) the correct description.

- [ ] There's a refrigerator. There are two lamps. There aren't any chairs.
- [ ] There's a sink and a stove. There are two chairs. There's a refrigerator.
- [ ] There's a sink and a stove. There's a washer and a fridge.

4 Look and write the prepositions.

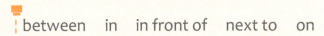

between   in   in front of   next to   on

1 

____________ the TV

2 

____________ the wall

3 

____________ the chairs

4 

____________ the box

5 

____________ the chair

5 Look and complete the sentences.

1. ____________________ a sofa.
2. ____________________ two chairs.
3. ____________________ a table.
4. ____________________ any lamps.
5. ____________________ a television.
6. ____________________ any photos.

6 Unscramble the questions.

1. is / a / bathroom / shower / there / in / the / ?

____

2. there / on / are / plates / table / the / ?

____

3. in / is / there / a / dryer / the / laundry room / ?

____

4. is / fridge / kitchen / there / a / in / the / ?

____

Just for Fun

1 **Read and solve the puzzle.**

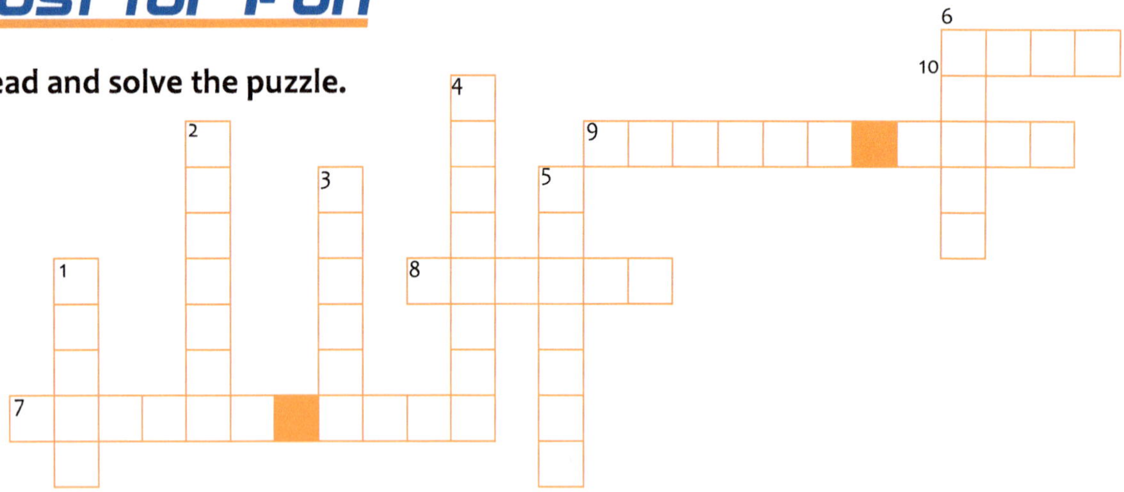

Down

1. One person can sit on this furniture.
2. You prepare food in this room.
3. You wash your clothes in this appliance.
4. You can shower in this room.
5. You sleep in this room.
6. You cook food with this appliance.

Across

7. You eat in this room.
8. Food is cold in this appliance.
9. You relax in this room.
10. Three people can sit on this furniture.

2 **Find, circle and describe five errors.**

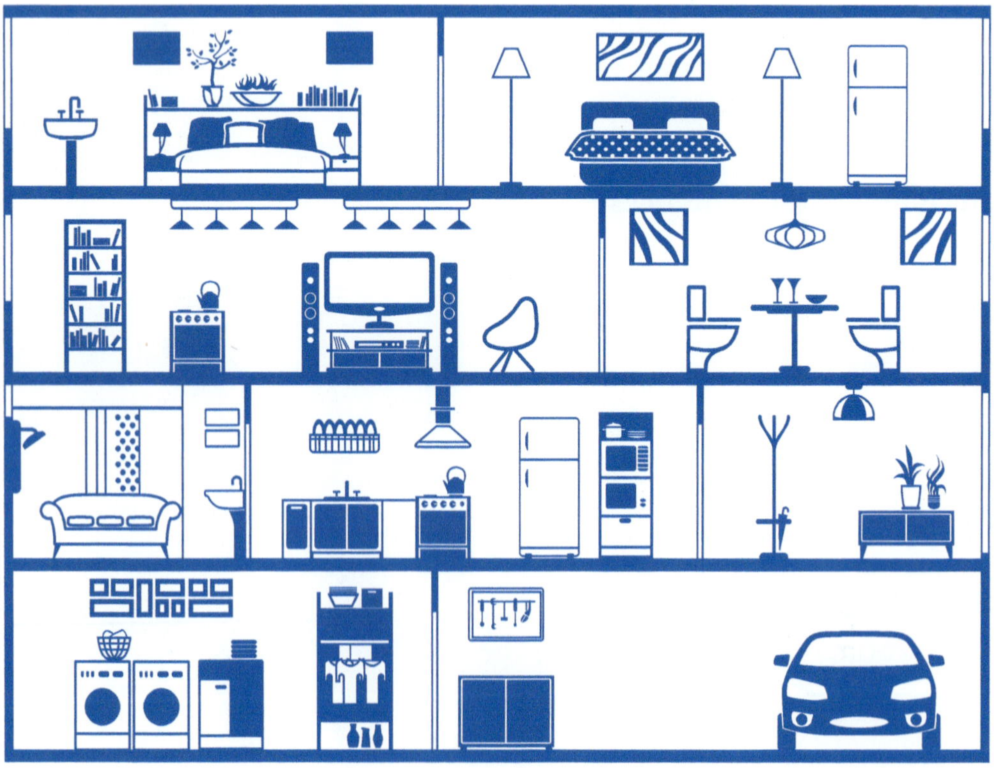

____

____

____

____

____

5

What's your routine?

Vocabulary

Lisa's Morning Routine

1 26 **Listen and number the scenes of the comic.**

2 26 **Listen again and match.**

1. wake up
2. take a shower
3. eat breakfast

4. get dressed
5. go to school

3 Read and complete the sentences.

one
school
six
thirty

Lisa's Afternoon Routine

1

I **eat lunch** at ______________ o'clock.

4 Think Fast! In your notebook, write eight sentences about your routine. (5 min)

2

After ______________, I **do my homework.**

3

At ______________ o'clock, I **eat dinner.**

4

At nine ______________, I **brush my teeth.**
Then I **go to bed.**

Guess What!
We use a.m. to talk about times in the morning and p.m. to talk about times in the afternoon and evening.

seven o´clock → 7 **a.m.** / 7 **p.m.**

Grammar

1 **Look and complete the comments using adverbs of frequency.**

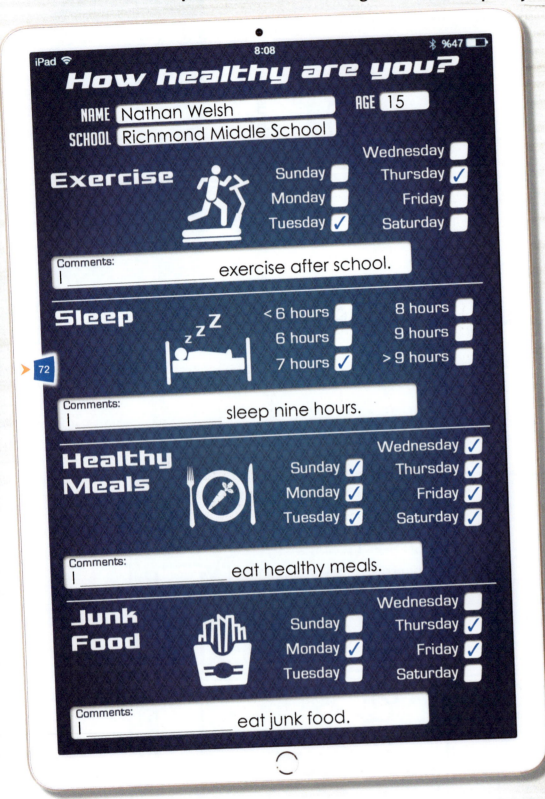

iPad 8:08 %47

How healthy are you?

NAME Nathan Welsh AGE 15

SCHOOL Richmond Middle School

Exercise

Sunday	☐	Wednesday	☐
Monday	☐	Thursday	☑
Tuesday	☑	Friday	☐
		Saturday	☐

Comments:
I ________ exercise after school.

Sleep

< 6 hours	☐	8 hours	☐
6 hours	☐	9 hours	☐
7 hours	☑	> 9 hours	☐

Comments:
I ________ sleep nine hours.

Healthy Meals

Sunday	☑	Wednesday	☑
Monday	☑	Thursday	☑
Tuesday	☑	Friday	☑
		Saturday	☑

Comments:
I ________ eat healthy meals.

Junk Food

Sunday	☐	Wednesday	☐
Monday	☑	Thursday	☑
Tuesday	☐	Friday	☑
		Saturday	☐

Comments:
I ________ eat junk food.

Adverbs of Frequency

always	✓✓✓✓✓
sometimes	✓✓✓XX
never	XXXXX

Present Simple, +

he / she / it
↓
verb + -s or -es
↓
eats, watches

I / you / we / they
↓
base verb form
↓
eat, watch

Guess What!
Breakfast, lunch and dinner are *meals*. In the United States, dinner is the biggest meal of the day.

2 **In your notebook, write about Nathan using adverbs of frequency.**

1. exercise 2. sleep 3. healthy meals 4. junk food

30 sec **3** **Think Fast!** Write four sentences about you.

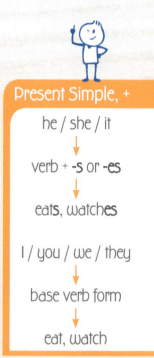

4 Look and number the dialogues. Then complete the dialogues.

1

2

3

4

5
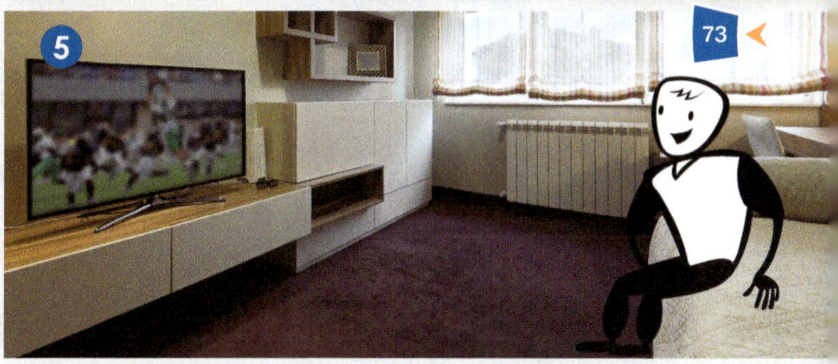

Present Simple, - and ?

he / she / it
↓
does / doesn't watch
↓
Does he watch TV?

I / you / we / they
↓
do / don't watch
↓
Do you watch TV?

- Samson Stickman ________ (exercise) a lot! ☐
- ________ (sleep) nine hours at night? — No, he doesn't. ☐
- Samson sometimes ________ (eat) junk food. ☐
- Does he watch TV in the evening? — Yes, ________. ☐
- He always ________ (eat) a healthy lunch. ☐

3 min 5 Think Fast! Unscramble the questions in your notebook. Then look and write the short answer.

1. you / healthy / a / breakfast / have / always / do / ? → ✗
2. parents / your / the / gym / to / do / go / ? → ✓
3. have / afternoon / do / P.E. / the / we / in / ? → ✗
4. your / sister / play / does / basketball / ? → ✗
5. school / does / their / have / pool / a / swimming / ? → ✓

Guess What!
It is also common to say *have* breakfast, lunch or dinner. You can also *have* a snack.

Westgate Community Center

Username Password Log In

Classes | About us | Membership | Location | Contact us!

New Art and Fitness Classes!

Yoga

Improve your health with yoga!

Monday
4:00 – 5:30 p.m.

Wednesday
6:15 – 7:45 p.m.

Minimum age: 15

Guitar

Learn to play the guitar!

Monday and Wednesday
4:00 – 5:30 p.m.

*For **beginners***
Minimum age: 12

Art for Adults

Express yourself with art for adults!

Tuesday and Thursday
11:00 a.m. – 12:30 p.m.

Saturday
9:30 a.m. – 12:30 p.m.

Minimum age: 18

Tai Chi

Are you **stressed**? Try tai chi!

Monday and Thursday
5:30 – 7:00 p.m.

Saturday
9:00 – 10:30 a.m.

Minimum age: 15

Photography

Learn techniques from an expert!

Friday
7:00 – 8:30 p.m.

Minimum age: 18

Cooking

Learn techniques from a professional!

Monday
9:00 – 10:30 a.m.

Thursday
6:00 – 7:30 p.m.

Minimum age: 18

Karate

Learn self-defense and discipline! All levels are welcome!

Tuesday
6:30 – 8:00 p.m.

Friday
8:15 – 9:45 p.m.

Minimum age: 6

Keep Fit! for Seniors

Join our exercise group for **seniors**!

Monday and Wednesday
9:00 – 10:00 a.m.

Minimum age: 60

For more information, call (555) 865-4663, or email us at healthyu@westcc.com.

Our National Feeds

Home FAQ Support Ask for more References

1 Read the information in the website and circle the correct option.

1. There are karate classes in the...
   a) morning. b) afternoon. c) evening.
2. The minimum age for cooking classes is...
   a) 15. b) 18. c) 16.
3. The *Keep Fit! for Seniors* class is...
   a) 90 minutes. b) 30 minutes. c) one hour.
4. The photography class is only on...
   a) Tuesdays. b) Fridays. c) Saturdays.
5. The yoga classes start at...
   a) 4:00 and 5:30 p.m. b) 4:00 and 6:15 p.m. c) 4:30 and 6:00 p.m.

Guess What!
We use prepositions to talk about time: *at* 6:00 *on* Tuesdays *from* 4:30 *to* 5:30.

1 min

2 Think Fast! Find a class for each person.

1. Mike is 16. He loves music.
2. Janet is 65 and she **wants** to exercise.
3. Dave is 21. He has a new camera.
4. Oscar is 35. He wants to learn to cook.

3 27 **Listen and complete the registration forms.**

1

Name	Carlie Smith		
Age		Class	
Days			
Time	____:____ - ____:____		

2

Name	Justin Carter		
Age		Class	
Days			
Time	____:____ - ____:____		

3

Name	Michelle Esposito		
Age		Class	
Days			
Time	____:____ - ____:____		

Be Strategic!
Before a conversation, think about the questions other people will ask you.

Glossary
fitness: health and physical condition
improve: to make something better
beginner: a person who is starting to learn something
stressed: tense or anxious
join: to participate in something
want: to have a desire

4 Choose a class for yourself.

Stop and Think! How can an art or fitness class improve a person's health?

Culture

1 Look at the map. Then read and circle the correct option.

1. Finland is in northern Europe / Asia.
2. It is very hot / cold in December.
3. It has a small / large **population**.

Finland has a **population** of 5.4 million people. They speak Finnish, or *Suomi*.

In Finland, winter is very cold, -30°C in some areas. In some regions, there are 51 days with no sun.

Ice hockey is very popular in Finland. There is also *pesäpallo*, a game that is similar to baseball. Skiing is also very popular.

There are 2.2 million saunas in Finland. In a sauna, people put water on hot rocks to create **steam**. Many families use the sauna every day.

Finland is a great place to see the aurora borealis, or the northern **lights**.

Finns eat lots of fish. They also eat potatoes, bread and cakes. They sometimes eat reindeer **meat**.

2 Read and complete the table.

Population	
Language	
Winter	
Saunas	
Foods	
Sports	

3 [28] **Listen and match.**

Finland's population of 5.4 million is very small. Here are the populations of some other countries:

China	49.5 million
The US	4.5 million
South Korea	330 thousand
New Zealand	1.4 billion
Iceland	300 million

4 Read and guess. Write *T* (True) or *F* (False) in the box.

1. Finland has 100,000 lakes. ☐

   ____

2. In the summer, the sun shines for 24 hours. ☐

   ____

3. The national animal is the polar bear. ☐

   ____

4. Finland is famous for its heavy metal music. ☐

   ____

5 [29] **Listen and check. Then correct the false sentences.**

Stop and Think! Why do you think saunas are popular in Finland?

Glossary

population: the number of people in a place

steam: water in the form of a gas

lights: (sing. light) a source of illumination

meat: flesh from an animal as food

Project

1 Circle the activities using the color code.

school sports other

2 Look at Cheryl's routine on page 79. Then circle *T* (True) or *F* (False).

1. Cheryl has a guitar class on Wednesdays at 4:30. T F
2. She goes to the gym on Tuesdays and Thursdays. T F
3. She has lunch with her grandma on Sunday. T F
4. She does chores on Saturday morning. T F
5. Her favorite TV series is on Thursdays at 7:45. T F
6. She goes shopping on Sunday afternoons. T F

3 Make an agenda with your weekly routines.

1. Make a list of your weekly routines.
2. Include school, sports and other activities.
3. Write the routines and times on your agenda.
4. Tell a classmate about your weekly routines: *I have breakfast at...*

November
Cheryl's
Agenda
MON
TUES
WED
THU
FRI
SAT
SUN
7:00 a.m.
7:30
8:00
8:30
9:00
9:30
10:00
10:30
11:00
11:30
12:00 p.m.
12:30
1:00
1:30
2:00
2:30
3:00
3:30
4:00
4:30
5:00
5:30
6:00
6:30
7:00
7:30
8:00
8:30
9:00
9:30
10:00
school
lunch
lunch with Grandma
do homework
pizza night!
favorite TV series!

Review

1 Read and match. Then look and number the photos.

1. Tim eats	at 6:00 a.m. every day.
2. My parents get up	to school by bus.
3. My little sister brushes	a shower in the mornings?
4. I sometimes go	lunch at 1:30.
5. Do you take	her teeth five times a day.

2 Look and complete.

1

______________ breakfast

2
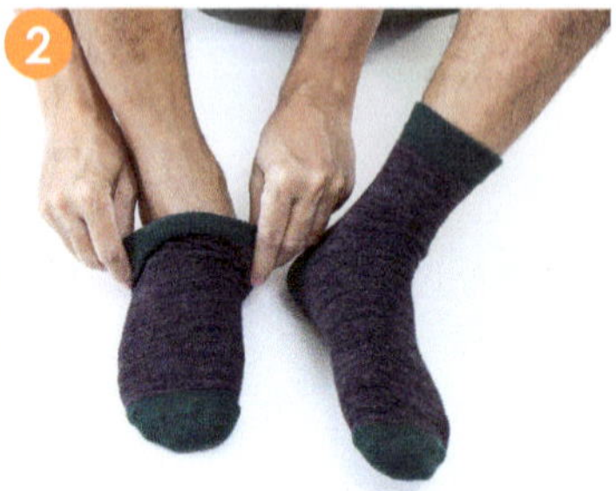
______________ dressed

3

do ______________

4

eat ______________

3 Look and circle the correct option.

1. 7:00 It's seven oh / o' clock.
2. 12:15 It's a quarter to / past twelve.
3. 4:30 It's half past / to four.
4. 11:45 It's a quarter past / to twelve.
5. 8:25 It's eight twenty- / thirty- five.
6. 10:15 It's a quarter to / past ten.

4 Look and circle *T* (True) or *F* (False).

1

2

3
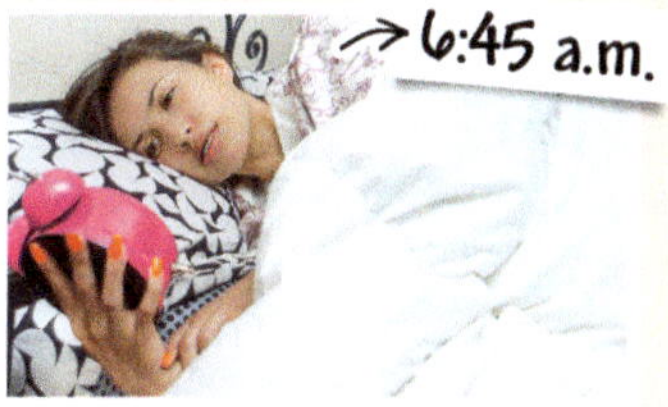

4

1. We eat dinner at half past six.	T	F
2. Amy does her homework at one o'clock.	T	F
3. Tara wakes up at half past six.	T	F
4. Zack and Alex go to bed at a quarter to nine.	T	F

5 Write sentences using *never*, *sometimes* and *always*.

1. They / eat breakfast (✗✗✗✗✗)

____

2. my mom / go to the gym / in the morning (✓✓✓✗✗)

____

3. I / watch TV / after school (✓✓✓✗✗)

____

4. my uncle / play tennis / on Saturdays (✓✓✓✗✗)

____

5. we / go to school / by bus (✗✗✗✗✗)

____

6 Complete the sentences using the correct form of the verb.

1. My dad ______________________ (not play) soccer.
2. ____________ you ____________ (go) to the gym? No, I ____________ .
3. ____________ Mike ____________ (wake up) early? Yes, he ____________ .
4. I ____________ (not eat) a lot of junk food.
5. ____________ they ____________ (watch) a lot of TV? Yes, they ____________ .

7 Read and correct the sentences.

1. Sam don't exercise a lot. ______________________________
2. Do you play basketball? Yes, I play. ______________________________
3. My friends not go to the gym. ______________________________
4. Natalia sometimes eat snacks. ______________________________
5. Does he get up early? No, he don't. ______________________________
6. What sports you play? ______________________________

Just for Fun

1 Decode the sentences. Then guess and circle the occupation.

a	b	c	d	e	f	g	h	i	j	k	l	m
n	o	p	q	r	s	t	u	v	w	x	y	z

1. v u n i r q v a a r e n g u n y s c n f g r v t u g.

2. v g n x r n f u b j r e n a q t r g q e r f f r q n g a v a r c. z.

3. v t b g b j b e x n g g r a g u v e g l.

4. v s v a v f u j b e x n g f r i r a v a g u r z b e a v a t.

5. v u n i r o e r n x s n f g n g u n y s c n f g f r i r a.

Who am I?

a farmer

a doctor

a P.E. teacher

6

How important is technology to you?

Vocabulary

1 🎧30 **Listen and number.**

84 **2** 🎧30 **Listen again and circle *T* (True) or *F* (False).**

1. Maggie thinks the phone is **complicated.** T F
2. She has a lot of **apps** on her phone. T F
3. She thinks the **screen** is small. T F
4. She uses her phone on the bus. T F
5. She can't make phone calls. T F

3 Read and complete the sentences.

check listens make send share surf watches

1. Maggie uses her phone to ____________ the Internet.
2. She can ____________ phone calls and ____________ messages.
3. She also ____________ to music and ____________ movies.
4. She uses one app to ____________ photos with other people.

Glossary

share: to send the photo, document or article via text, e-mail or social network

complicated: difficult to use or understand

apps: applications; computer programs

screen: the area for text and images on a TV, computer, or phone

30 sec **4 Think Fast!** Look and identify the functions of the devices. What can you do with them?

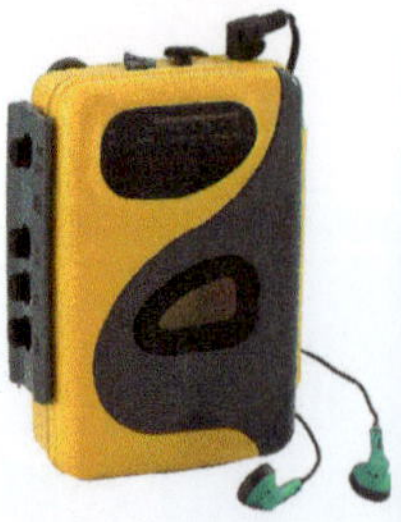

5 Read and complete the e-mail.

https://www.mail.com/Maggie_inbox

Home

Compose | Reply | Save | Print | Delete | Maggie

Inbox (1)

Sent items

Saved items

Trash

To: Veronica Palitos <veronica75@stickmail.com> cc/Bcc

Subject: How to write e-mails

Dear Aunt V,

Here are some tips for your new e-mail account!

Click the ______ button to keep important e-mails. These go in the "Saved items" folder.

Click ______ to respond to an e-mail. The new e-mail goes back to the sender.

To make a paper version of an e-mail, click ______. This is only for important e-mails.

To put an e-mail in the trash, click ______. Use it for junk mail and old messages.

To write a new e-mail, click ______.

I hope this helps!

Love,
Maggie

Send

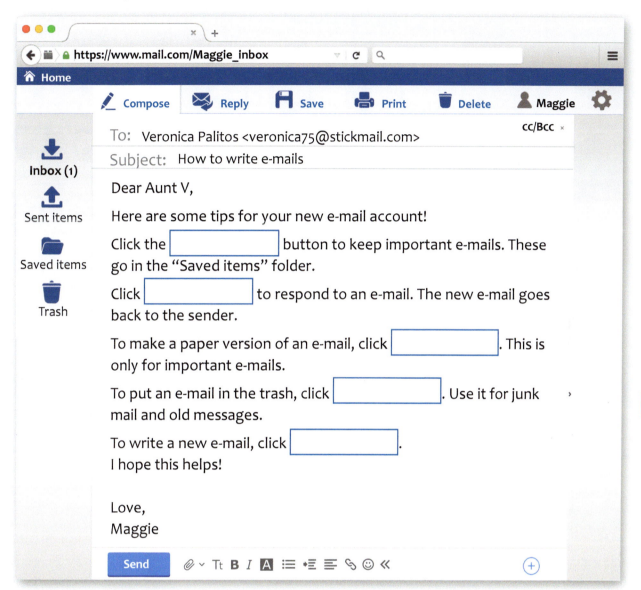

6 Read and match.

1. save	a new e-mail
2. delete	a paper copy
3. compose	to an e-mail
4. print	important messages
5. reply	junk mail

30 sec

7 Think Fast! Say the e-mail addresses.

1. karlie.g@bigmail.com
2. soccerboy99@supermail.net
3. jane.bowser@myschool.edu
4. ethan.jones@protectanimals.org

Guess What!

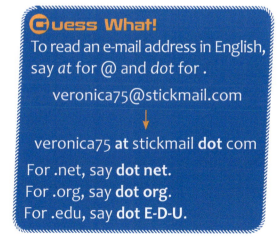

To read an e-mail address in English, say *at* for @ and *dot* for .

veronica75@stickmail.com

↓

veronica75 **at** stickmail **dot** com

For .net, say **dot net.**
For .org, say **dot org.**
For .edu, say **dot E-D-U.**

Grammar

1 Look and complete using a frequency expression.

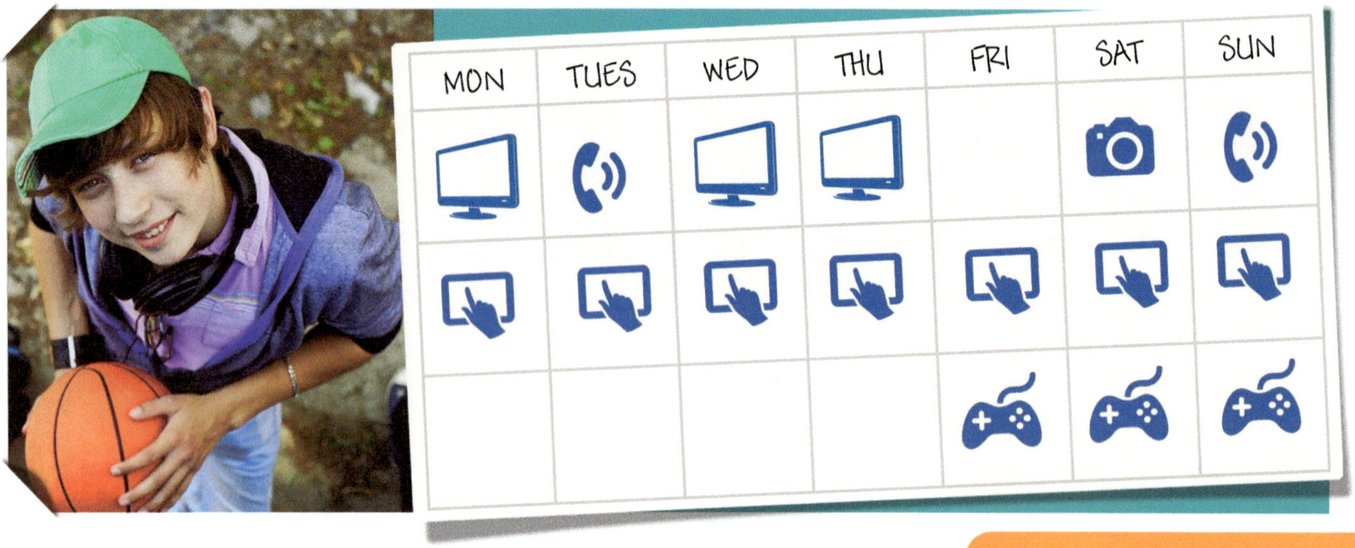

1. James watches TV ______________________.
2. He takes photos ______________________.
3. He surfs the Internet ______________________.
4. He makes phone calls ______________________.
5. He plays games ______________________.

Frequency Expressions

MON, TUES, WED, THU, FRI, SAT, SUN
→ every day

MON, TUES, WED
→ three times a week

MON, THU
→ twice a week

MON
→ once a week

2 Write the frequency expressions on the chart.

every day   once a month   once a week
three times a week   twice a day   twice a year

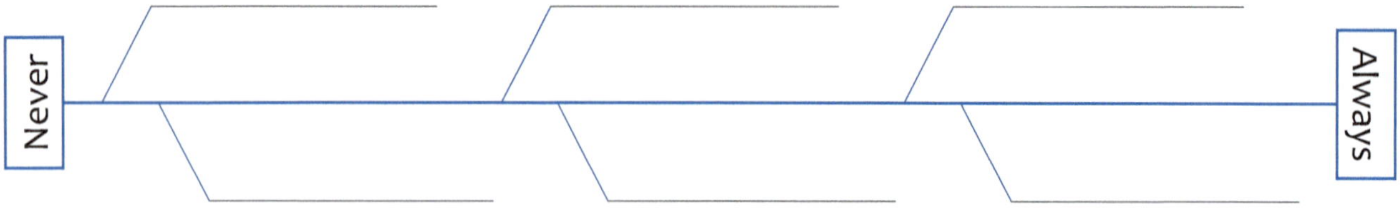

3 31 Read the questions. Then listen and circle the correct option.

1. Does James make phone calls every day? Yes, he does. / No, he doesn't.
2. Does he listen to music every day? Yes, he does. / No, he doesn't.
3. Do his friends send him messages every day? Yes, they do. / No, they don't.

4 Think Fast! In your notebook, write five sentences about your habits.

5 Read and complete using the questions words.

online

__________ do you play basketball?

At the community center.

Write message

online

__________ do you watch movies?

Twice a week.

Write message

online

__________ is your sister's name?

It's Kate.

Write message

online

__________ do you watch movies?

On Saturdays and Sundays.

Write message

online

__________ do you share photos with?

With my friends.

Write message

Question Words

- What?
- Where?
- Who?
- When?
- How often?

Guess What!
It is common to call questions with question words *Wh-questions* because most of the words begin with *wh*: **what, when, where, who.**

6 Unscramble and match.

1. do / what / have / games / you / ?
   ____
2. you / volleyball / do / play / where / ?
   ____
3. when / you / movies / do / watch / ?
   ____
4. who / take / you / do / photos of / ?
   ____

My friends and my mom.

In the evenings.

At school.

FIFA 2016 and Mario Kart 8.

5 min

7 Think Fast! Choose three questions. Ask and answer with a classmate.

1. what time / do your homework?
2. how often / send messages?
3. what / your dad's name?
4. where / take photos?
5. what / favorite food?
6. when / play games?

Reading and Writing

1 Read and match the questions with the actions.

1. What does "inbox" mean?
2. What is my doctor's phone number?
3. Where is 253 Water Street?
4. When can I see *Pirates of the Pacific 3*?
5. Who is the President of France?

- find an **address**
- look up **facts**
- find contact information
- find a definition
- look up movie times

2 Read and complete the sentences.

technology

You can use **lowercase** letters. To a search engine, "technology" is the same as "TECHNOLOGY."

~~226 Oke Streat~~ 226 Oak Street

Spelling is important! Search engines depend on correct spelling. They can only correct minor spelling errors.

president ~~of the~~ united states

Don't use punctuation or words like *a*, *the* or *of*. Search engines focus on key words.

math game algebra

Be specific. The Internet has a lot of information. Add key words to limit the search results.

"I have a dream"

Use quotation marks for exact phrases.

Be Strategic!
Key words are nouns and action verbs. Focus on key words to find the main idea of a sentence.

1. Use ______________ letters.
2. Correct ______________ is important.
3. Don't use ______________.
4. Use ______________, not *a*, *the* or *of*.
5. Add ______________ to limit the search results.

Guess What!
The three most popular search engines are Google, Bing and Yahoo.

3 Write search terms for each topic.

1. Where is 1600 Pennsylvania Avenue? ______________
2. What is the capital of Australia? ______________
3. What is the origin of the quotation, "That's one small step for a man"? ______________
4. What are the **lyrics** to the Beatles' song, "Hello, Goodbye"? ______________
5. What is the temperature in the Sahara Desert? ______________
6. What is the translation of "hello" in Turkish? ______________

Stop and Think! How can you find **reliable** information on the Internet?

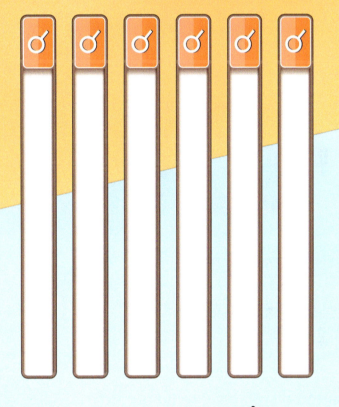

Glossary

address: the location of a place
facts: information that is true
lowercase: small letters; *a*, *b*, *c*–not *A*, *B*, *C*
lyrics: words of a song
reliable: something you can believe or trust

Culture

NAME
Canada, from the Iroquois word for "village"

CAPITAL
Ottawa

POPULATION
35 million people

OFFICIAL LANGUAGES
English and French

OTHER LANGUAGES
- more than 50 indigenous languages
- six forms of sign language

FLAG
red and white bars with a red maple leaf in the center

FAMOUS FOODS
- maple syrup (for hotcakes)
- poutine (French fries with cheese and gravy)

OTHER FACTS
- The Royal Canadian Mounted Police, or "Mounties," wear red uniforms with a red coat and a brown hat.
- Many video games are from Canada, such as FIFA, Prince of Persia and NBA Live.

1 Read and answer the questions.

1. The name "Canada" is from an Iroquois word. What does it mean? ____________________
2. Canada has two official languages. What are they? ____________________
3. The Canadian flag is red and white. What is in the center? ____________________
4. Poutine is a popular Canadian dish. What's in it? ____________________
5. Canadian Mounties (police officers on horses) are famous for their uniforms. What color are their coats? ____________________
6. Some popular video games are from Canada. What is one example? ____________________

2 Read the descriptions. Who are the famous Canadians?

1. He sings and writes pop songs. He's famous for the hit song *Baby*.
2. She's a famous actor. You can see her in *Juno*, *Inception* and *X-Men*.
3. He's an actor. He's famous for movies like *The Truman Show* and *Horton Hears a Who*.

Answers: 1. Justin Bieber 2. Ellen Page 3. Jim Carrey

3 32 Listen and number the cities.

3 32 Listen again and match.

1. Toronto	has ranches and rodeos.
2. Vancouver	is a very small town.
3. Montreal	is good for golf.
4. Calgary	has a lot of Italian immigrants.
5. Iqaluit	has underground museums.

Stop and Think! Are there people from different cultures in your country? What do you know about their cultures?

Project

1 Read and mark (✓). Where do you use your phone to do these activities?

	Home	School	Transportation	Restaurants
watch videos	☐	☐	☐	☐
listen to music	☐	☐	☐	☐
play games	☐	☐	☐	☐
send messages	☐	☐	☐	☐
take photos	☐	☐	☐	☐
make phone calls	☐	☐	☐	☐

2 Look at the technology infographic on page 93 and write the number.

How many people...

1. watch videos at school? ______
2. take photos at restaurants? ______
3. listen to music at home? ______
4. make phone calls on transportation? ______
5. send messages at school? ______
6. play games at home? ______

3 Make a class technology infographic.

1. Observe the people at home, at school, in stores and at restaurants.
2. Note the number of times a person does each activity.
3. Report your findings in a table.

	At home	At school	On transportation	At restaurants
watch videos	||		|||	
listen to music	|||	|	卌 ||	

4. Add the results from the entire class. Find a classroom total for each activity.

	At home	At school	On transportation	At restaurants
watch videos	47	3	36	5
listen to music	41	4	58	0

5. Make your infographic. Report the results on bar graphs.

USES of technology

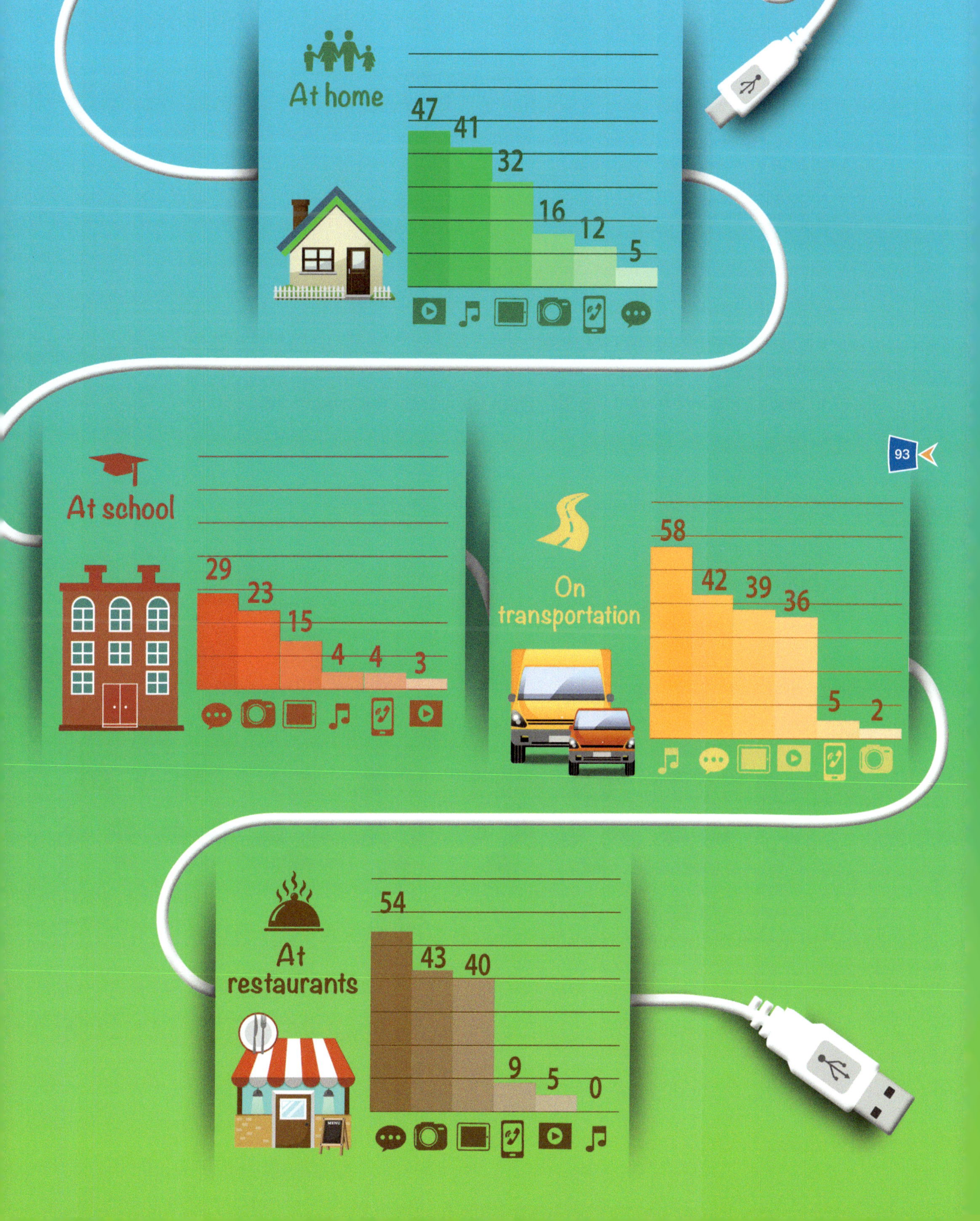

Review

1 Read and match.

1. watch
2. share
3. surf
4. listen
5. shop
6. make
7. check
8. send

photos | phone calls | to music | e-mail | online | the Internet | movies | messages

2 Find and correct the mistakes.

1. My sister always makes photos of her friends. ______________________
2. Can I make the phone call? ______________________
3. My friends listen of music on the bus. ______________________
4. My parents don't shop Internet. ______________________
5. Bill surfs games on his computer. ______________________

3 Find and circle five e-mail words. Then look and label the icons.

94

R A E S O P M O C Y
K W Q T T J V I K L
D R Q N E G E Y A P
X H I R R L P K V E
C R Y R K M E O A R
P C F S A V E D D C
U Y Y Z O P F R A U
D O P O U E H B O E

1. ______________________
2. ______________________
3. ______________________
4. ______________________
5. ______________________

4 Look, read and write the names.

	Mon	Tues	Wed	Thu	Fri	Sat	Sun
Max							
Vicky							
Zoe							

1. ______________________ shops online once a week.
2. ______________________ checks his/her e-mail on Fridays.
3. ______________________ doesn't watch movies on Saturdays.
4. ______________________ texts people three times a day.
5. ______________________ watches movies twice a week.
6. ______________________ listens to music every day.
7. ______________________ and ______________________ don't play video games.

5 Unscramble and match.

1. often / you / games / how / video / do / play / ? ____________________ In the dining room.
2. parents / movies / do / watch / what / your / ? ____________________ In the evening.
3. she / where / homework / does / do / her / ? ____________________ At the park.
4. photos / do / where / they / take / ? ____________________ Action movies.
5. send / you / do / messages / when / ? ____________________ Twice a week.

6 Complete and answer the questions.

1. Where ________ you ________ photos? ____________________
2. What ________ your favorite games? ____________________
3. When ________ you ________ to music? ____________________
4. Who ________ you send messages to? ____________________
5. How often ________ your parents ________ their e-mail? ____________________

7 Read the article and answer the questions.

Cory sends messages to his parents every day. He doesn't make a lot of phone calls. He plays games with his friends once a week at an Internet café. He watches basketball on TV twice a week. He also has an mp3 player and he listens to music in the evenings.

1. How often does he send messages?
____
2. Who does he send messages to?
____
3. Where does he play games?
____
4. What does he watch on TV?
____
5. When does he listen to music?
____

Just for Fun

1 Read and solve the puzzle.

Down ↓

1. ______________ a new e-mail
2. surf the ______________
3. ______________ photos
4. ______________ e-mail
5. play ______________
6. take ______________
7. ______________ to an e-mail
8. shop ______________

Across →

9. ______________ to music
10. ______________ a paper copy
11. watch ______________
12. ______________ junk mail
13. make a ______________
14. send ______________
15. make ______________ calls
16. ______________ an important e-mail

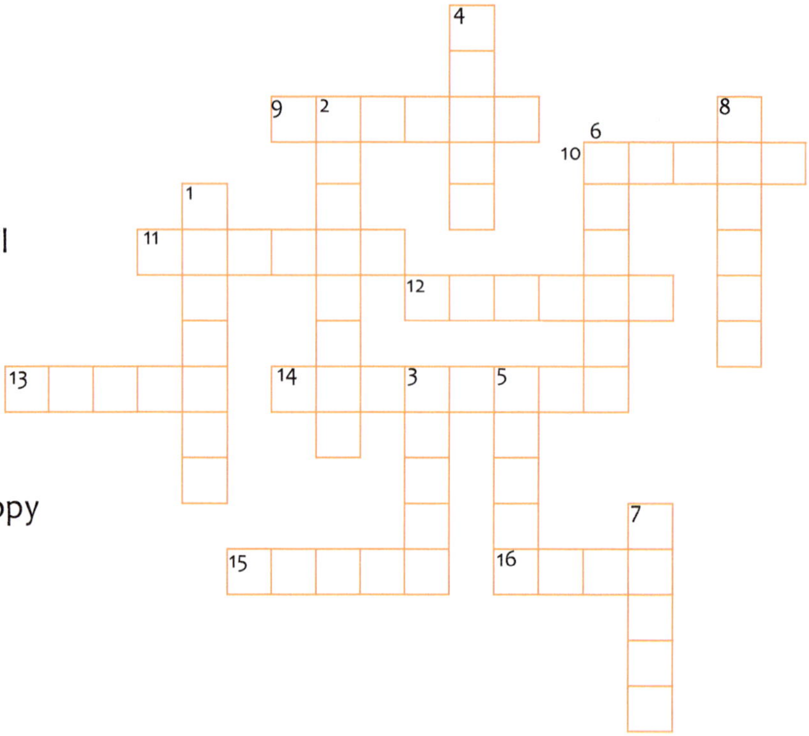

7

What are you wearing?

Vocabulary

1 **Read the blog and find the clothing items in the webpage of the week.**

Easy Fashion Tips

by Gaby Mitchells

HOME FACEBOOK INSTAGRAM CONTACT ME

Do you have the right clothing and accessories for every occasion?
There are certain items that should always be in your closet.

Jeans (1) are casual and comfy. You can wear them with a T-shirt (2) for casual events. Jeans can also **go with** a blouse (3) (for girls) and a shirt (4) (for **guys**) for a more elegant look.

For formal occasions, such as family dinners and other special occasions, girls should have a dress (5) or a black, gray or **navy** skirt (6), and a **pair of** elegant sandals (7) or **pumps**. For boys, a pair of black pants (8), a white shirt and a tie (9) is perfect. Black or brown shoes (10) complete the formal outfit. Formal clothing is expensive—not cheap—but it's essential. Look out for **sales**!

And if it is cool outside, make sure you have a sweater (11) and a jacket (12) or coat (13). Hats (14) and scarves (15) are **useful** accessories. Oh, and girls, don't forget boots (16) — they always look good, with jeans, dresses or skirts — even when it is **warm**!

About me

Subscribe

FOLLOW ME!

Fashion Webpage of the Week

HOME WOMEN MEN JUNIORS KIDS SHOES ACCESSORIES

MORE

12 COMMENTS

2 **Read and circle *T* (True) or *F* (False).**

1. Old boots go with a formal dress. T F
2. Blouses are for both boys and girls. T F
3. It is useful to have brown shoes in your closet. T F
4. T-shirts are formal. T F

2 min

3 **Think Fast!** In your notebook, write five items you have in your closet.

Glossary

go with: combine with
guys: boys or men
navy: very dark blue
pair of: a set of two
pumps: women´s shoes with a higher heel
sales: discounted prices
useful: helpful or practical
warm: not cold

4 Look and mark (✓) the item that doesn't belong.

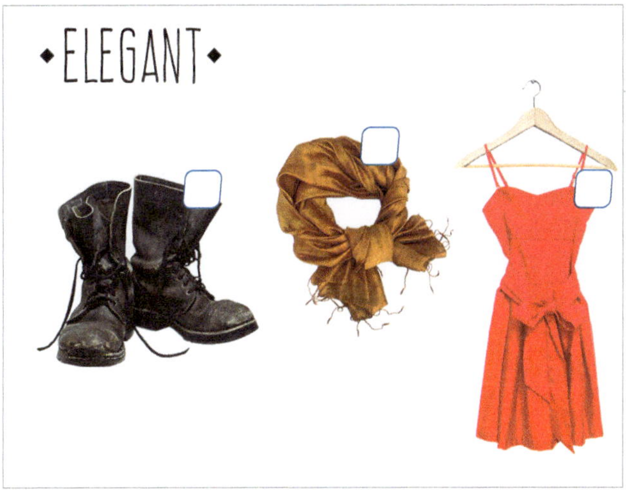

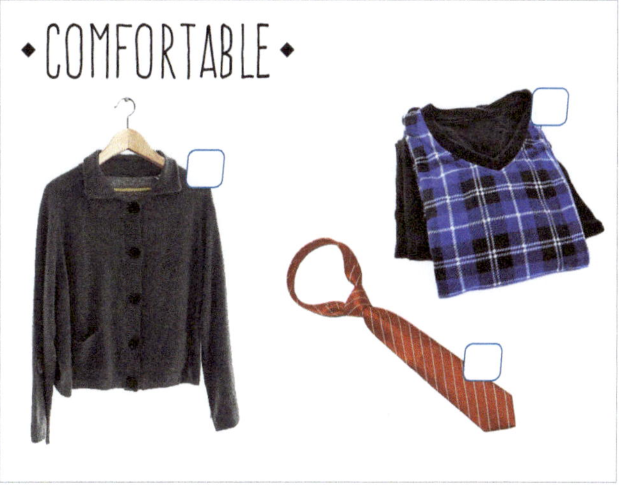

5 Read and circle the correct definition.

1. casual	informal / formal	3. cheap	costs a lot / doesn't cost a lot
2. elegant	simple / sophisticated	4. expensive	not elegant / not cheap

6 In your notebook, describe what they are wearing.

Guess What!
Jackets can be formal and elegant for both girls and guys. They can also be casual and warm to wear on cool days.

Grammar

1 Look and mark (✓) the activities in the comic.

skating ☐ dancing ☐ eating ☐ listening to music ☐ watching a movie ☐

studying ☐ singing ☐ texting ☐ taking photos ☐ playing games ☐

2 33 **Listen and number the scenes.**

3 33 **Listen again and label the characters in the comic.**

Anthony Lilly Melissa Trisha Paul Rose Thomas

Guess What!
"Say cheese!" is an expression people say so that they smile in a photo.

2 min **4 Think Fast! Look and write the names.**

1. He's wearing sunglasses and he's eating a sandwich. ____________
2. She isn't dancing. She's wearing jeans, a blouse and a hat. ____________
3. She's wearing a T-shirt. She's studying. ____________
4. He's wearing striped pants and he's taking photos. ____________
5. She's dancing. She's wearing a skirt and sweater. ____________

Guess What!
Watch out for spelling changes with present continuous verbs:
sit → sitting
dance → dancing

5 Read and complete the chart.

Present Continuous
be + action + *-ing*
We'________ singing.
She's study________.
They ________n't eating.

6 Read and circle the correct option.

1. He is / are taking photos.
2. They isn't / aren't doing homework.
3. You is / are wearing a new jacket!
4. Is / Are you watching a movie? No, I'm not.
5. Is / Are she making a video? Yes, she is.
6. What are you doing? I 'm / 's studying.

2 min **7 Think Fast!** In your notebook, write sentences using the cues.

1. I / not study
2. we / dance
3. she / wear / a blue dress
4. they / not wear / boots
5. you / do homework / ?
6. they / exercise / ?

Listening and Writing

1 Look at the photos and number the places.

- at the arcade ☐
- at the food court ☐
- at the mall ☐
- on the bus ☐
- at the movie theater ☐

2 [34] Listen and write the photo captions.

3 [34] Listen again and complete.

1. ______________ back already?
2. Look ______________ photos.
3. Oh, ______________ scary!
4. In ______________, we're playing video games.

Stop and Think! What do you share online? What is good to share? What isn't?

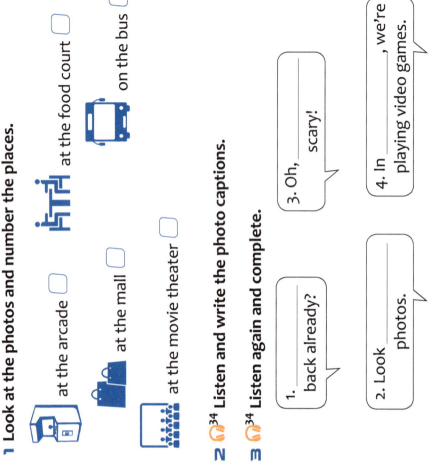

Be Strategic!
Adjectives add information to nouns: **beautiful** dress, **delicious** food. Use adjectives to make captions more interesting to your audience.

2 hours ago

11 likes

Like Comment Share

Jo Stickman _with Elsie
3 hours ago

5 likes 1 comment

Like Comment Share

Maggie: Mmm. Delicious!

Jo Stickman _with Elsie
4 hours ago

8 likes

Like Comment Share

4 Read and underline the adjectives.

1. We're having a great time!
2. Tim's studying for a hard exam.
3. I'm eating a delicious hamburger.
4. They're watching a funny movie.
5. I'm reading an interesting book.

5 Write sentences using the present continuous.

1. we / eat / some delicious pasta

____

2. I / make / long scarf

____

3. he / read / a great book

____

4. they / watch / a popular TV series

____

1 min 5 Think Fast! Describe the pictures using adjectives.

Culture

1 **Read and circle the correct option.**

Vietnam

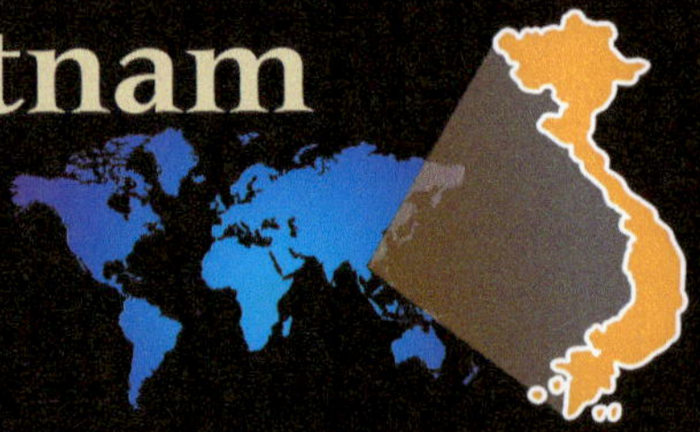

...is a small country with a large population. It is home to 93.7 million people.

Forty percent of all Vietnamese people have *Nguyen* as a family name.

It can be difficult to cross the street in Vietnam because there are 37 million motorbikes and only 2 million cars.

Many people wear a cone-shaped hat called a *nón lá* to protect them from the sun.

The **currency** in Vietnam is the *dong*.

A lot of Vietnamese children have pigs as pets.

The lunar calendar is important in Vietnamese culture. People use it to choose the date for their **weddings**.

1. The national currency of Vietnam is the...
   a. dong.
   b. yen.
   c. rubel.
2. ____________ are popular pets in Vietnam.
   a. Cats
   b. Dogs
   c. Pigs
3. In Vietnam, there are ____________ motorbikes, but only 2 million cars.
   a. 37 million
   b. 19 million
   c. 7 million
4. A nón lá is a type of...
   a. hat.
   b. pet.
   c. motorbike.
5. ____________ percent of Vietnamese people have "Nguyen" as a family name.
   a. Twenty
   b. Thirty
   c. Forty
6. People plan weddings according to the...
   a. lunar calendar.
   b. Chinese horoscope.
   c. weather.

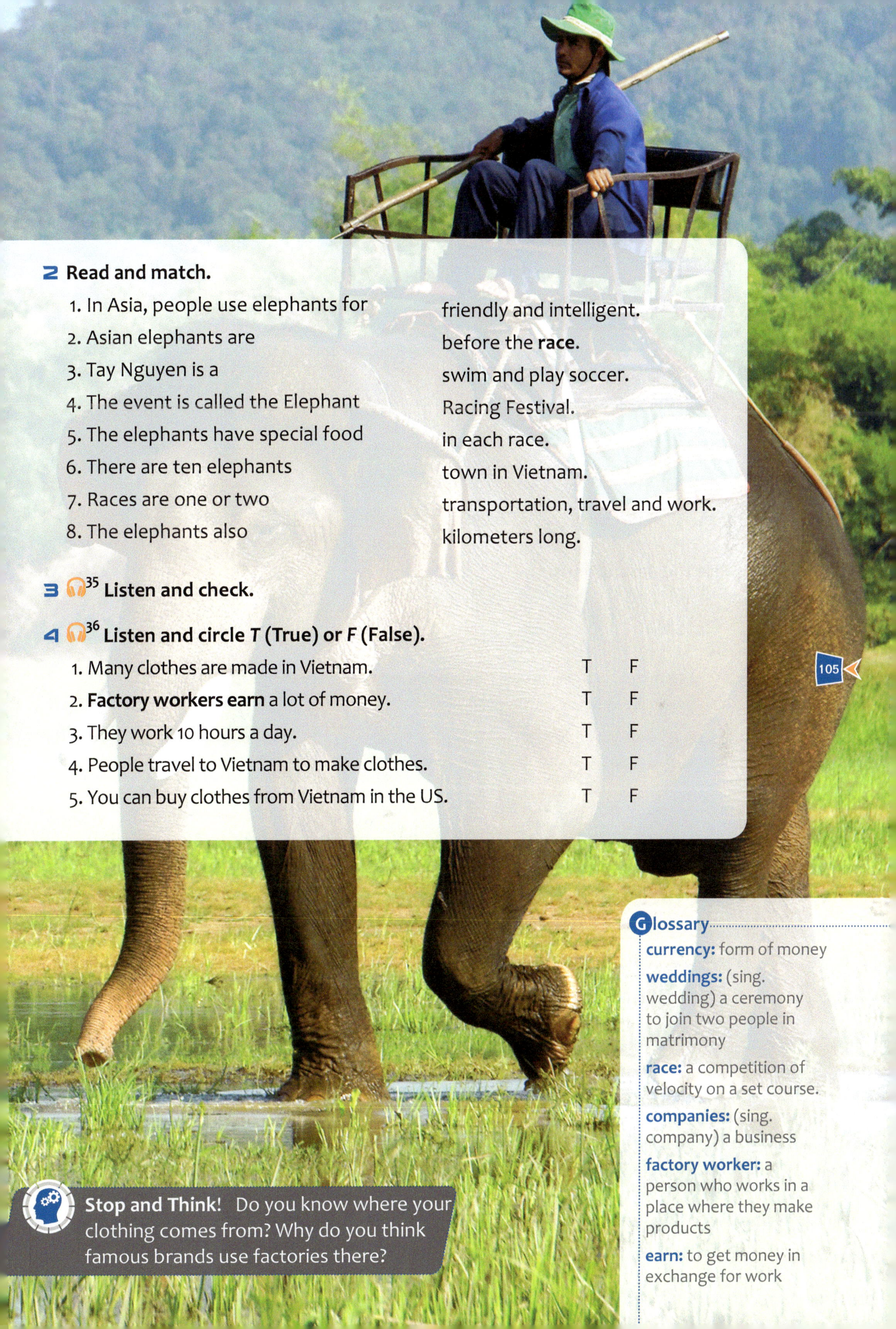

2 Read and match.

1. In Asia, people use elephants for	friendly and intelligent.
2. Asian elephants are	before the **race**.
3. Tay Nguyen is a	swim and play soccer.
4. The event is called the Elephant	Racing Festival.
5. The elephants have special food	in each race.
6. There are ten elephants	town in Vietnam.
7. Races are one or two	transportation, travel and work.
8. The elephants also	kilometers long.

3 35 Listen and check.

4 36 Listen and circle *T* (True) or *F* (False).

1. Many clothes are made in Vietnam.	T	F
2. **Factory workers earn** a lot of money.	T	F
3. They work 10 hours a day.	T	F
4. People travel to Vietnam to make clothes.	T	F
5. You can buy clothes from Vietnam in the US.	T	F

Stop and Think! Do you know where your clothing comes from? Why do you think famous brands use factories there?

Glossary

currency: form of money

weddings: (sing. wedding) a ceremony to join two people in matrimony

race: a competition of velocity on a set course.

companies: (sing. company) a business

factory worker: a person who works in a place where they make products

earn: to get money in exchange for work

Project

1 Classify the words.

comfortable skirt friend shirt dad green blue casual brother elegant white hat red shoes sister shorts grandma useful cool black

Colors	Adjectives	Clothes	Relationships

2 Complete the descriptions.

106

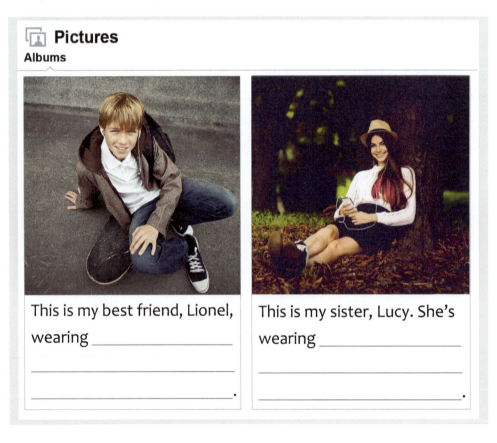

Pictures
Albums

This is my best friend, Lionel, wearing ____.

This is my sister, Lucy. She's wearing ____.

3 Make VIP (Very Important Person) Profiles for four or more people.

1. Choose people who are very important to you.
2. Find photos of the people.
3. Say who they are.
4. Describe what they are wearing.
5. Present your VIP profiles.

VIP Profiles

This is my friend, Avery. She's wearing a purple sweater and a red scarf.

This is my mom. She's wearing a black coat and a wollen scarf.

This is my friend, Tania. She's wearing a white blouse and jeans.

This is my grandpa. He's wearing a gray shirt and a warm sweater.

This is my teacher, Mr. Farrell. He's wearing a blue shirt, a red tie and jeans.

This is my big brother, Travis. He's wearing a gray shirt and shorts.

Review

1 Look and circle the correct option.

1 
T-shirt / blouse

2 
hat / tie

3 
sandals / socks

4 
boots / shoes

5 
scarf / tie

6 
dress / skirt

7 
pajamas / shorts

8 
sweater / pants

9 
jacket / coat

2 Classify the clothing items.

dress hat jeans pants scarf shoes shorts tie

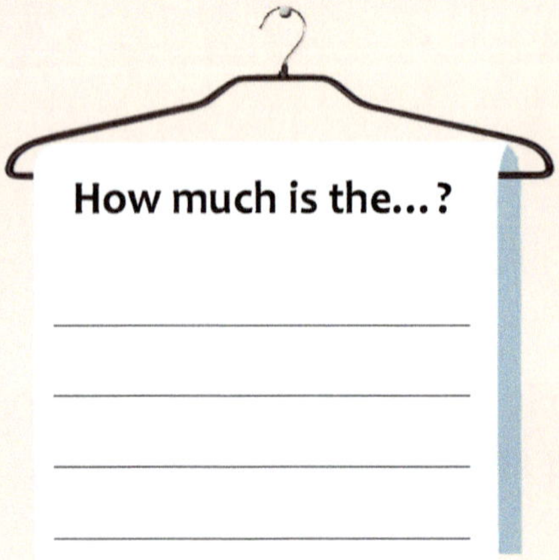

How much is the...?

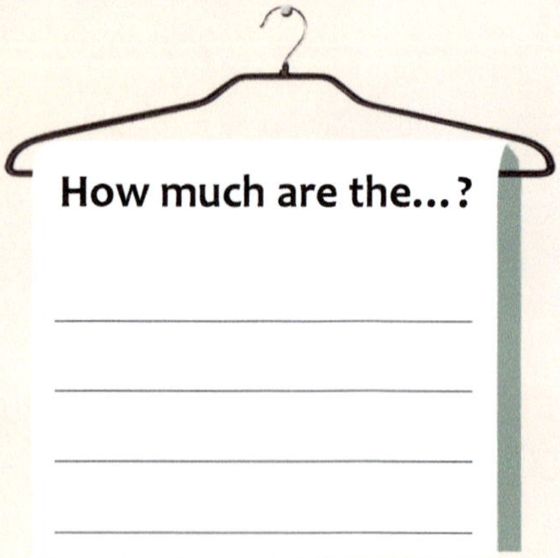

How much are the...?

3 Look and complete the prices.

1. $68.00 ____________-____________
2. $16.25 sixteen ____________-____________
3. $45.99 forty -____________ ninety-____________
4. $89.95 eighty-nine ____________-____________
5. $56.50 ____________-____________ fifty

4 Unscramble the adjectives.

1. aaclsu ____________________
2. folcabmorte ____________________
3. etelnga ____________________
4. envexepis ____________________
5. pheca ____________________
6. sueufl ____________________

5 Read and complete using *is* or *are*.

1. Oliver ____________ making a video at the party.
2. Kat and I ____________ eating lunch at the mall.
3. My cousins ____________ visiting my grandmother.
4. The cat ____________ sleeping on the sofa.
5. Jack ____________ reading an interesting book.

6 Complete the sentences using the present continuous.

1. My mother ____________________________ (study) French.
2. Jen ____________________________ (not wear) jeans today.
3. My friends ____________________________ (take) selfies.
4. I ____________________________ (not study).
5. We ____________________________ (listen to) music.
6. My grandpa ____________________________ (watch) a movie.

7 Unscramble and match.

1. are / friends / what / doing / your / ?
   ____ No, he isn't.
2. he / is / watching / movie / a / scary / ?
   ____ Playing soccer.
3. are / how / you / doing / ?
   ____ Her mom.
4. a / wearing / new / Fiona / coat / is / ?
   ____ I'm fine, thanks.
5. who / texting / is / she / ?
   ____ Yes, she is.

8 What are they wearing? Look and describe using colors and adjectives.

____
____
____
____
____
____
____

____
____
____
____
____
____
____

Just for Fun

1 **Look and identify the items in the collage. Write their names on the lines.**

1. ______________
2. ______________
3. ______________
4. ______________
5. ______________
6. ______________
7. ______________
8. ______________

What do they have in common?

____

____

2 **Read the clues and mark (✓) one item each person is wearing.**

	a blue T-shirt	a gray sweater	red shoes	brown boots
Sam				
Charlie				
Jess				
Anna				

Clues:

The boys are wearing black shoes.

Charlie isn't wearing gray clothing.

Sam is cold.

Jess isn't wearing boots with her dress.

Anna doesn't like red.

The girls look very elegant.

2 min **3** **Think Fast!** Make a similar puzzle and give a friend to solve.

8

What do you love doing?

Vocabulary

1 **Look at the photos. What kind of vacation is it?**

Sea Adventures

*offers a lot of options for you to spend time **on land** or **at sea**!*

Classes

Take a cooking (1) class in your free time! We have two experts on board: Yashimi Harukami, a sushi master from Kyoto, and Paolo Castanella, a pizza chef from Rome.

We also offer yoga classes for beginners and experts. Raj is a yoga instructor with many years of experience.

Or go to one of our gyms—we have three!—and lift weights (2) or use our **exercise equipment**!

2

Go swimming (3) in our saltwater pool.

3

1

112

Exercise

Go climbing (4) on our climbing wall! There is one **on deck**, outside in the sun!

4

Play miniature golf (5) or volleyball with friends!

5

2 **Read and identify the activities in the brochure.**

3 **Read and underline the correct meanings.**

1. lifting weights	a. doing exercise to be strong	b. doing exercise to be faster
2. snorkeling	a. swimming underwater to see fish	b. floating in water to relax
3. waterskiing	a. moving on skis behind a boat	b. looking at fish from a boat
4. surfing	a. activity of making boats	b. traveling across water on a board
5. climbing	a. moving fast to a place	b. moving up a mountain or rock

▸ On Land

Sea Adventures stops in several ports. You can go shopping (9) for souvenirs or listen to **live music** or relax on the beach where you can get a tan (8).

You can do water sports as well: snorkeling (7), waterskiing (10) and surfing (6) with instructors is available!

▸ Onboard Entertainment

And in the evening, you can eat at different restaurants, go to the movies or see a show! There is also a salsa club for our dancers!

4 Complete the e-mail using the correct verbs.

go (2X) going see play take

Dear Grandma,

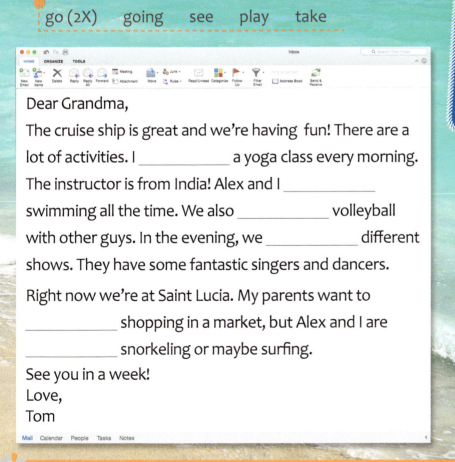

The cruise ship is great and we're having fun! There are a lot of activities. I ___________ a yoga class every morning. The instructor is from India! Alex and I ___________ swimming all the time. We also ___________ volleyball with other guys. In the evening, we ___________ different shows. They have some fantastic singers and dancers.

Right now we're at Saint Lucia. My parents want to ___________ shopping in a market, but Alex and I are ___________ snorkeling or maybe surfing.

See you in a week!
Love,
Tom

Guess What!
We use *go* for many activities: *go swimming*. We also use *play* for many sports: *play volleyball*.

Glossary

on land: not on a boat or in water

at sea: on a boat in the ocean

on deck: on the outside level of a boat or ship

exercise equipment: machines and devices that help with exercise

live music: music played by a band; not a recording

3 min **5 Think Fast!** Spell words from the e-mail for a classmate to guess.

Grammar

1 **Look, read and circle the correct option.**

2 **Write sentences about Jo's family using the clues.**

1. Dad / fish

____

2. Mom / fish

____

3. Jo / camping

____

4. Owen / go to the bathroom in the woods

____

Likes and Dislikes

love/s ☺
like/s ☺
don't/ doesn't like 😐
hate/s ☹
+ verb + *–ing*

3 37 **Listen and circle *T* (True) or *F* (False).**

1. The weather is perfect for swimming. T F
2. Jo's sisters don't like fishing. T F
3. Owen wants to go shopping. T F
4. They all hate hiking. T F

4 37 Listen again and mark (✓). What does the Stickman family decide to do?

go fishing ☐

go hiking ☐

go shopping ☐

go swimming ☐

Let's...

We use *Let's* to make suggestions.
Let's listen to music.
Let's go swimming!

5 **Match the comments and the suggestions.**

1. I love salsa dancing.	Let's take some classes.
2. I'm **hungry**.	Let's watch a different one.
3. This movie is boring.	Let's go shopping.
4. I want a new dress.	Let's go dancing on Friday.
5. I can't swim.	Let's eat some sushi.

5 min

6 **Think Fast!** Write five suggestions for the weekend using *Let's*.

1. ____________________
2. ____________________
3. ____________________
4. ____________________
5. ____________________

Glossary

woods: a place outside the city with a lot of trees; forest
fresh: not polluted
trail: a marked path through the woods
hungry: when you want to eat something

Listening and Reading

1 38 **Listen and complete the facts.**

1. There are ____________ million islands in the world. Most of these islands are **uninhabited** because they are very small.
2. ____________ million people live on islands. That's approximately one out of every ____________ people on Earth!
3. Java is the most populated island. ____________ million people live there. There are also many islands with a small population.
4. Australia is the biggest island! It has ____________ million square kilometers.

2 39 **Listen and mark (✓). What is on Palmerston Island?**

Stop and Think! What are the advantages and disadvantages of living on a **remote** island?

Be Strategic!
Listen for place value words and decimals in large numbers.

four **hundred** → 400
ten **thousand** → 10,000
three **million** → 3,000,000
two **point** four million → 2.4 million

3 Read and complete the sentences.

I love living on this island. It's a cool place and people are friendly. There are so few of us, we are like one big family. Life on the island is different from life in the city. In the morning, my friends and I go to school like other kids all over the world, but in the afternoon, we work: we **grow** vegetables, go fishing and collect **coconuts**. We only have electricity for six hours in the morning and six hours at night! There are many things to do in our free time. I love going surfing and snorkeling!

1. The people on Palmerston Island are ________________.
2. Kids on Palmerston Island ________________ in the morning.
3. William ________________ after school.
4. People only have ________________ for twelve hours a day.
5. William loves ________________ in his free time.

4 Complete the chart. How is life on Palmerston Island similar to / different from life where you live?

On Palmerston Island	Where I live

Glossary

uninhabited: no people live there

remote: very far away

grow: to take care of plants, often to produce food

coconuts

Culture

Russia

1 How much Russian do you know? Look and label.

- balalaika
- blini
- matryoshka
- troika

1 тройка

....

118

2 балала́йка

....

2 🎧40 Listen and check. Then practice saying the Russian words.

3 🎧41 Listen and circle the correct option.

1. There are __________ matryoshka dolls in a set.
   a. five b. seven c. ten
2. On a troika, you need a warm...
   a. coat. b. dress. c. lunch.
3. A troika is a…
   a. cart. b. boat. c. sled.
4. You can eat blini with **jam** or…
   a. caviar. b. salad. c. meat.
5. People can play in balalaika…
   a. orchestras. b. festivals. c. restaurants.

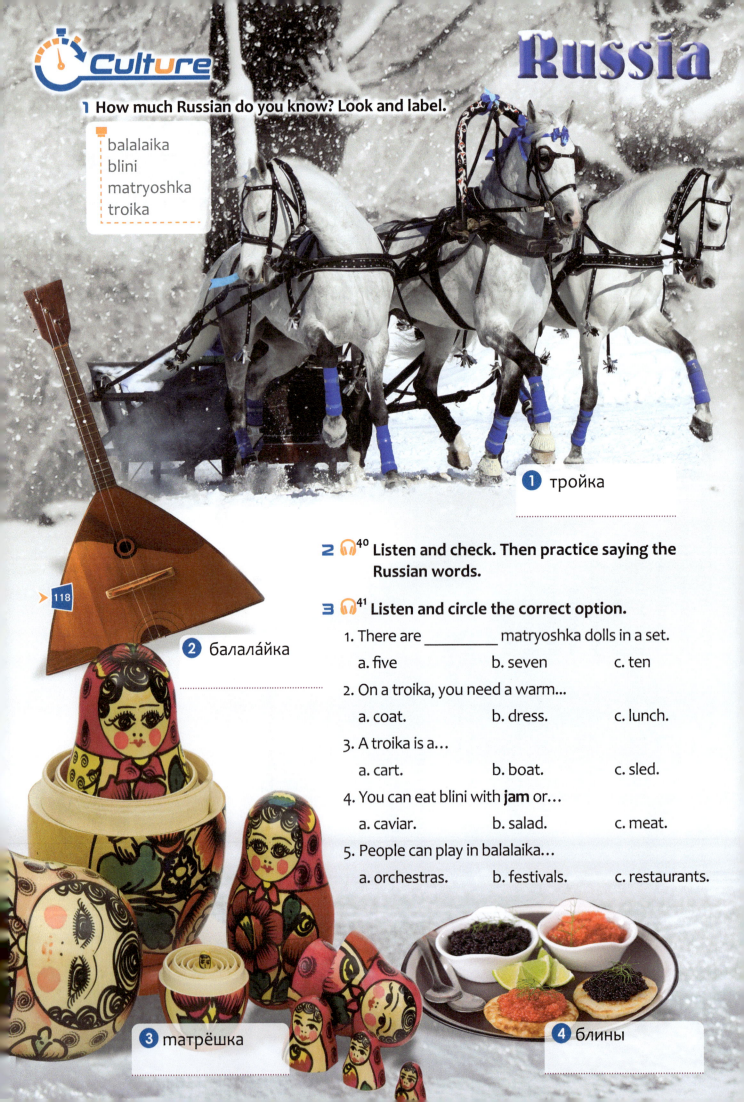

3 матрёшка

....

4 блины

....

4 Look and underline. What is the topic of the text?

a. Russian landscapes   b. Winter festivals   c. Indoor activities

5 Read and underline the parts you find interesting.

In Russia, the winters are very long and cold. In the north, there is sometimes **snow** for five months. Winter is also a time of many festivals. January 1st is New Year's Day. In Russia there are eleven time zones—so people can see the arrival of the new year eleven times! The **first** city to welcome the new year is Anadyr in Siberia. New Year's traditions in Russia are similar to Christmas traditions in other countries. People decorate a tree, and *Ded Moroz* (Father Frost) and *Sneguroshka* (Snow Maiden) bring presents! On January 19th, the Orthodox Church celebrates *Epiphany*. Some **brave** people celebrate that day by swimming in **freezing** water. It can be as cold as -25° Celsius! Russians love going to winter festivals, singing traditional **songs** and dancing. They love making ice **sculptures**, too. Some are really beautiful!

Glossary

jam: fruit preserves

snow: frozen white precipitation

first: 1st; the ordinal form of 1

brave: not afraid; valiant

freezing: extremely cold; the temperature at which water becomes ice

songs: music with words you can sing

sculptures: figures created by artists

6 Find and underline these items in the text.

1. weather in winter
2. number of time zones
3. a city in Siberia
4. two traditional characters
5. a religious event

Stop and Think! Do you like observing traditions? What is your favorite tradition?

Project

1 Read and mark (✓) activities you love doing.

Indoor Activities		Outdoor Activities	
Watching movies	☐	Swimming	☐
Reading	☐	Volleyball	☐
Cooking	☐	Miniature golf	☐
Eating out	☐	Fishing	☐

2 42 Listen and complete the missing information.

SURVEY

Vacation activities

Personal data

Name:

Age: 14 City: Miami

☺

😐

☹ eating out

SURVEY

Vacation activities

Personal data

Name: Donna Blues

Age: 14 City:

☺ taking classes, reading

😐

☹

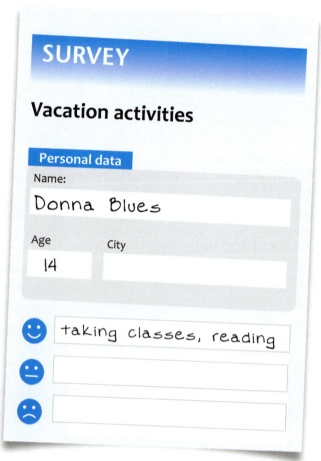

3 42 Listen again and complete the questions.

1. What's ______________________?
2. Where ______________________?
3. What ______________________?
4. Which activities ______________________?
5. Which ones ______________________?
6. Which ______________________?

4 Make a survey about vacation activities.

1. Choose four outdoor and four indoor vacation activities.
2. Interview five friends or family members using the questions in Activity 3.
3. Record the interviews.
4. Present the results. Use the poster on page 121 as an example.

FREE-TIME ACTIVITIES

Participants	Age	City
1. Donna Blues	14	London
2. Sam Smith	14	Miami
3. Nat Mora	15	Madrid
4. Simon Paget	15	Vancouver
5. Rakel Johanson	14	Stockholm

INDOOR

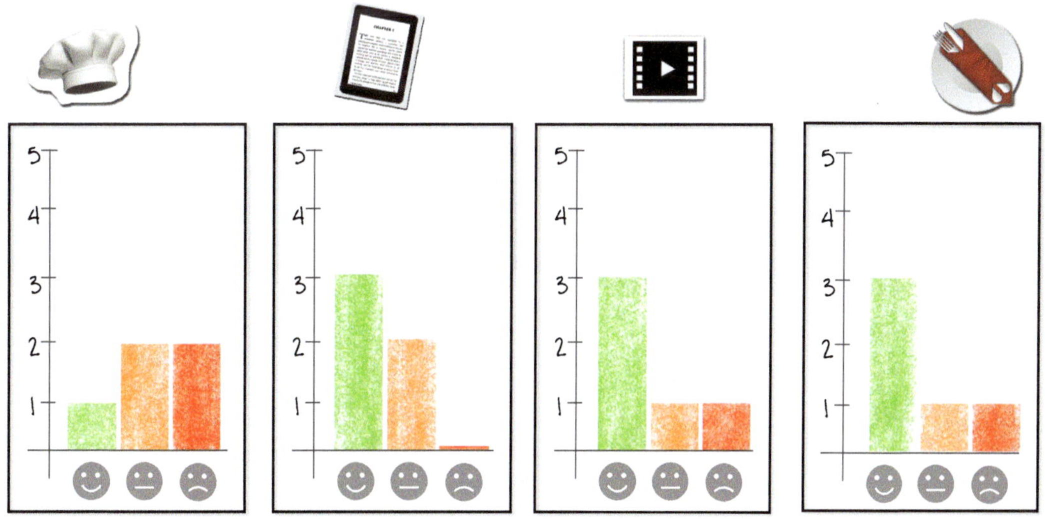

OUTDOOR

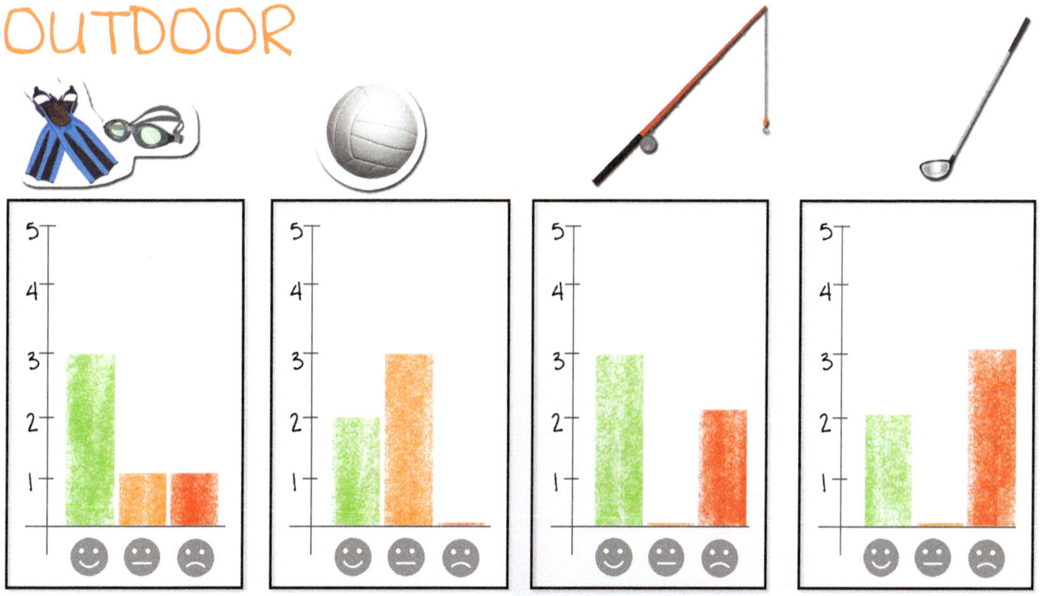

Review

1 Read and match.

1. lift weights
2. play miniature golf
3. cook
4. go shopping
5. go surfing
6. go waterskiing
7. go climbing
8. get a tan
9. go swimming
10. go snorkeling

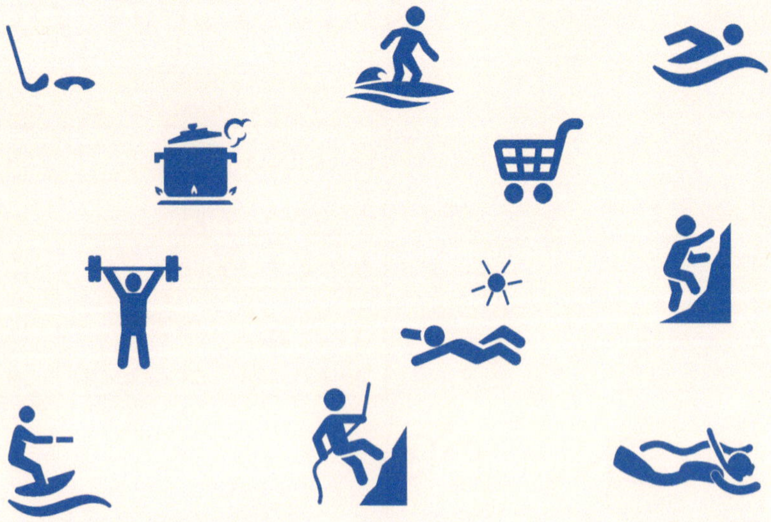

2 Make a list. Which activities do you do in water?

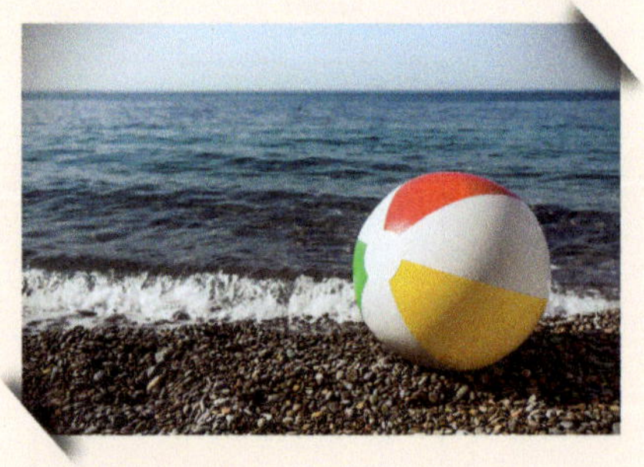

____

____

____

____

3 Read and solve the puzzle.

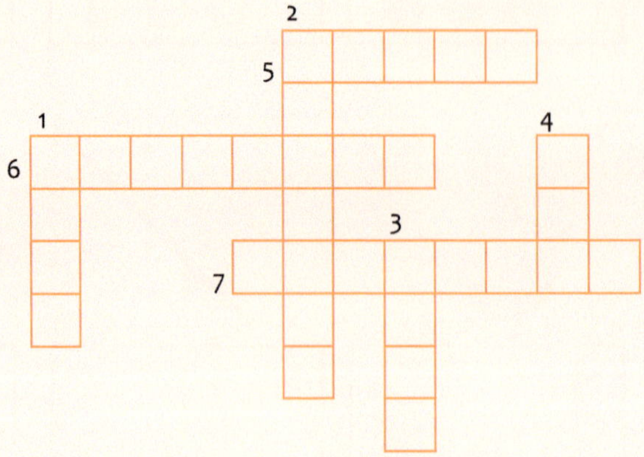

Down ↓

1. You do this to prepare food.
2. You can lift these in a gym.
3. You use this verb with sports.
4. You can get this in the sun.

Across →

5. You go swimming in this.
6. You do this to move up a mountain.
7. You can do this at a mall.

4 Look and complete the sentences. Then number the photos.

1. She hates ______________________ homework.
2. He loves ______________________ books.
3. They like ______________________ to music.
4. They like ______________________ video games.

5 Read and number the lines of the dialogue.

OK, no swimming. Do you like climbing? They have a climbing wall at the gym.

Great! Let's go!

The community pool is open. Let's go swimming.

Hi, Dawn. What are you doing?

Hmm. I don't like swimming.

Oh, I love climbing!

I'm watching TV.

Just for Fun

1 Look and connect the letters. Then write the phrases below using the correct verbs.

124

1. ______________________
2. ______________________
3. ______________________
4. ______________________
5. ______________________
6. ______________________
7. ______________________
8. ______________________
9. ______________________
10. ______________________

Workbook

1 Unit

Vocabulary – Family Relationships

1 Look and write the name.

Who am I?

0. Beth is my sister. Veronica
1. Jason is my brother. ______________
2. Paul is my father. ______________, ______________
3. Sara is my cousin. ______________, ______________

2 Decode the new words: 1=a, 2=b, 3=c…

0. Owen is Bill's s o n. 19-15-14
1. Sara is Veronica's _ _ _ _ _. 14-9-5-3-5.
2. Ron is Maggie's _ _ _ _ _. 21-14-3-12-5
3. Sara is Beth's _ _ _ _ _ _ _ _. 4-1-21-7-8-20-5-18
4. Chris is Beth's _ _ _ _ _ _. 14-5-16-8-5-23

Possessive 's

Use 's after a noun to indicate possession:

the sister of Sara → Sara's sister

the aunt of Owen → Owen's aunt

the dad of Chris → Chris's dad

3 Write the word.

0. a short word for "mother" mom
1. a short word for "father" ______________
2. mother and father ______________
3. a short word for "grandmother" ______________
4. a short word for "grandfather" ______________
5. grandmother and grandfather ______________

4 Find and write eight family words.

G R A N D M A L E L R A U N T E H N D Q
S O N I I U Y V G A O N N V L S J I A Z
W F K T Z Q A P P O K U C R O J S E D B
M S T X H C T L A L E F L D A P G C L F
D A U G H T E R Q W B N E I W B W E T X
F M W B Q Y W I G C O U S I N P L T V D

grandma ______________

______________ ______________

______________ ______________

______________ ______________

Grammar – Demonstratives

1 Look and circle the correct option.

This / These are my cousins.

That / This is my mom.

This / These is my house.

That / This is my grandpa.

These / Those are my sisters.

That / This is my nephew.

2 Read and match.

1. this + that
2. these + those
3. this + these
4. that + those

nearby 

plural 

far 

singular 

Possessive Adjectives

3 Complete the chart.

Subject Pronouns	Possessive Adjectives
I	my
	your
he	
	her
it	
	our
they	

4 Replace the phrase with a possessive adjective.

0. ~~My sister's~~ name is Julie.
   Her name is Julie.
1. **My father's** name is Bob.
   ____
2. **My brothers'** names are Leo and Matt.
   ____
3. **My grandma's** name is Leonora.
   ____

5 Complete the sentences.

0. (me + Ann) Our names are Sam and Ann.
1. (me) ____________ name is Pablo.
2. (James) ____________ name is James.
3. (Max + Tim) ____________ names are Max and Tim.
4. (you) What is ____________ name?

Guess What!
When a noun is singular, add 's. When a noun is plural, add ' after the s: my brothers' names.

1 Unit

Verb *be*

6 Look and write the sentences.

I	he / she / it	you / we / they
am	is	are

0. Alicia / my aunt
   Alicia is my aunt. — Is Alicia ______ your aunt?
1. Nathan / my brother
   ______ — ______ your brother?
2. Simon and Alex / my cousins
   ______ — ______ your cousins?
3. That / my cat
   ______ — ______ your cat?
4. These / my parents
   ______ — ______ your parents?

Guess What!
To form *Yes-No* questions, put the verb *be* before the subject:
Is Isabel your mother?
Are Sam and Ian your cousins?

7 Complete the questions in Activity 6.

Review

1 Read and correct the sentences.

0. ~~These~~ is my sister, Katie.
   This is my sister, Katie.
1. Those are my brother, Tyson and Chad.
   ______
2. Our name is Peter.
   ______
3. My sister name's is Renee.
   ______
4. Hugo is your uncle?
   ______
5. Is they your brothers?
   ______

2 Complete the table.

male	female
grandfather	grandmother
	grandma
parent	
	aunt
son	
	cousin
brother	
	mother
dad	
	niece

Reading

1 Look at the pictures and circle the correct answer.

1. What is the text about?
   a. pandas
   b. chimpanzees
   c. gorillas

2. Where do they live?
   a. in Africa
   b. in Antarctica
   c. in Asia

2 Read and complete the notes.

CHIMPANZEES AND HUMANS: ARE WE RELATED?

Quick facts

- Chimpanzees live in Africa. Their habitat is mostly forests. They live in and around trees.
- Chimpanzees weigh from 25 to 50 kilograms. They live up to 50 years.
- Their diet is mixed. They eat fruit and plants (80%) and meat (20%).

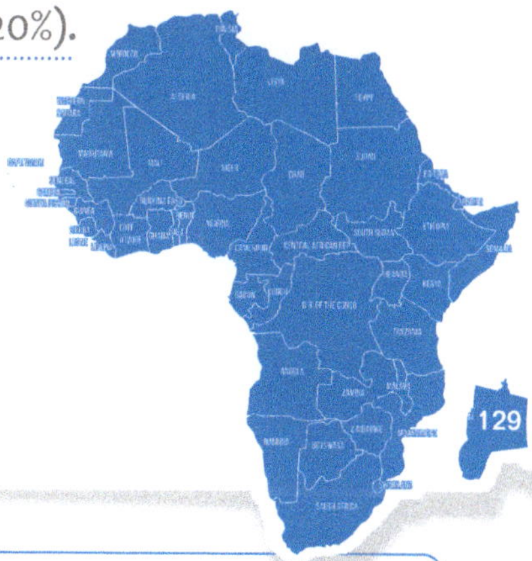

Family life

Humans and chimpanzees are both social animals. Chimps live in big families, with 10 to 100 individuals! Chimpanzees are social and intelligent.

Genetics

Humans also share DNA with *all* living beings. We share 98% of our DNA with chimpanzees.

Habitat in and around trees	**Weight**
Diet	**Longevity**

3 Read and circle the correct animal.

Habitat
They live in the world's oceans.

Diet
They eat fish and squid.

20 **Longevity**
They live up to 20 years.

Size
They are 2–4 meters long.

Fun Fact
They can jump 4 meters high.

2 Unit

Vocabulary – School Subjects and Places

1 Look and write the school subjects.

0  ______

1  ______

2  ______

3  ______

2 Write the short forms of the words.

0. physical education P.E.
1. laboratory ______
2. mathematics ______
3. gymnasium ______

Guess What!
In middle school, students study **science** subjects such as **physics, chemistry** and **biology.**

3 Classify the school words.

School Subjects
history

School Places

~~history~~ laboratory geography music room physics biology science math cafeteria classroom chemistry library auditorium

Grammar – Indefinite Articles

1 Number the objects in alphabetical order. Then write *a* or *an*.

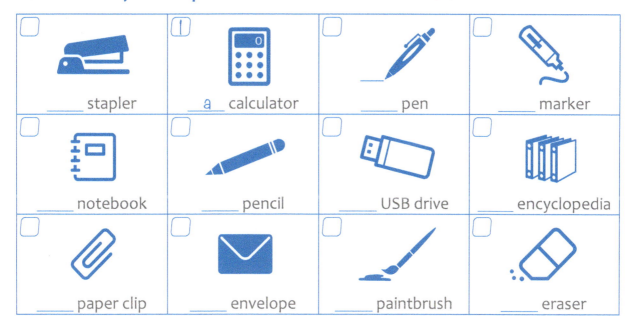

☐  ____ stapler	☐ 1  __a__ calculator	☐  ____ pen	☐  ____ marker
☐  ____ notebook	☐  ____ pencil	☐ 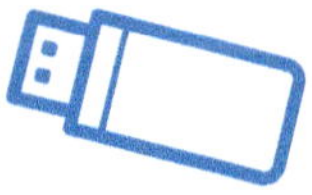 ____ USB drive	☐  ____ encyclopedia
☐  ____ paper clip	☐  ____ envelope	☐  ____ paintbrush	☐  ____ eraser

Verb *have*

2 Write the subjects under the correct verb forms.

I   Chris and Pete   Lisa   Paul
The teacher   Tim and I   You

have / don't have

I
____
____
____

has / doesn't have

____
____
____

Guess What!
The words *don't* and *doesn't* are contractions:
do + not ⟶ **don't**
does + not ⟶ **doesn't**

3 Read the schedule and complete the sentences.

0. Bailey __has__ math in the morning.
1. She ______________ art in the morning.
2. Bailey and Mia ______________ English together.
3. Bailey ______________ history in the afternoon.
4. She ______________ chemistry this year.
5. She ______________ volleyball after school.

Bailey's Schedule
In the morning (8:00-12:00)
math
P.E.
English—with Mia!!!
biology

In the afternoon (12:00-3:00)
lunch
history
art
technology

After school (3:00-5:00)
volleyball

4 Write the questions.

0. Mia + Bailey / technology/ together?
   Do they have technology together?
   No, they don't.
1. Bailey / biology / in the morning?
   ____
   Yes, she does.
2. she / math / at 8:00?
   ____
   Yes, she does.
3. Bailey / music / this year?
   ____
   No, she doesn't.

5 Complete the chart.

Short Answers with *do*			
Yes, I do.	Yes, he ______.	Yes, you do.	Yes, they ______.
No, I ______.	No, he ______.	No, you ______.	No, they don't.

Prepositions

6 Look and complete the sentences.

in next to on under

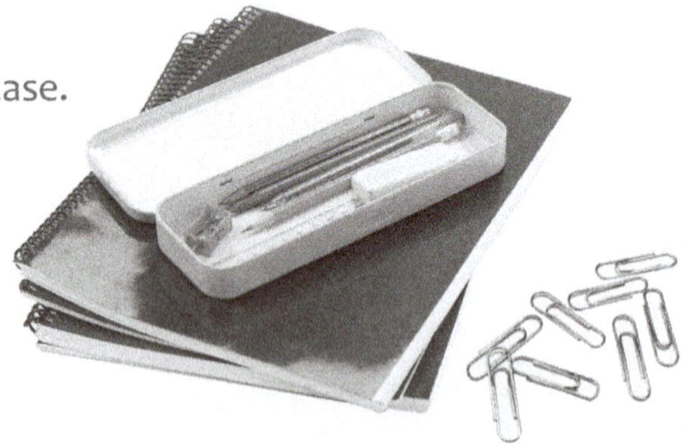

0. The pencil sharpener is in the pencil case.
1. The eraser is ______ the pencils.
2. The pencil case is ______ the notebooks.
3. The notebooks are ______ the pencil case.
4. The eraser is ______ the pencil case.
5. The paper clips are ______ the notebooks.

Review

1 Read and circle the correct option.

0. Mike has (a) / an soccer game after school.
1. Sara doesn't have a / an tablet.
2. The school has a / an nice cafeteria.
3. My school is next to a / an big university.
4. Do you have a / an extra pencil?
5. Does Martin have a / an mp3 player?

2 Look and rewrite the sentences.

0. Dennis has an exam this morning. → ? Does he have an exam this morning?
1. Lilly and Sophie have karate at 4:00. → - ______________________
2. I have physics with Ms. Jones. → - ______________________
3. Matt has lunch in the cafeteria. → ? ______________________

Writing

1 Read and number from 1 to 4 (1 = most important, 4 = least important).

modern school **installations** ☐

good teachers ☐

a **variety** of courses ☐

sports and physical education ☐

2 Read and complete the chart.

Homeschooling
Is it a good alternative?

In homeschooling, students don't go to a school. They study **at home**.

Their parents are the teachers.

They study the same school subjects as traditional students.

They can go to museums.

They can also take music or P.E.

They take exams **like** traditional students, too.

Homeschooling	Traditional Schools
	P.E. and team sports

3 Imagine that you study at home. In your notebook, make a schedule for your school day.

Glossary

installations: useful features of a place

variety: with many options

at home: the place where you live

like: similar to

3 Unit

Vocabulary – Countries and Nationalities

1 Unscramble the names of the countries. Then match the countries and the nationalities.

0. urep — Peru	British
1. sarautial ______	Indian
2. tpeyg ______	Egyptian
3. nutide modgnik ______	Peruvian
4. diani ______	Brazilian
5. zaribl ______	American
6. nitued tastes ______	Chinese
7. anhic ______	Australian

Guess What!
The term **Latin America** describes Spanish- and Portuguese-speaking countries in North and South America.

2 Find and write the nationalities.

France Greece Italy Japan Thailand Turkey

134

Q J I T A L I A N Q P V
D A A Z U H F T M S F G
P P H O X R E R L G S R
C A T E L I K G E K Y E
A N S A N L A I I N V E
E E U M A P E W S E C K
R S H K N B R F A H X H
G E G S E V N P W V M Y

Italian
______
______
______
______
______
______

3 Look and write the nationalities.

0. 
Italian

1. 
______

2. 
______

3. 
______

4. 
______

Grammar – Verb *be*

1 Look and complete.

0. I + am = I'm
1. you + ______ = ______
2. she + ______ = she's
3. we + are = ______
4. ______ + ______ = they're

2 Write the contractions.

0. Mike **is not** British. **He is** Australian. isn't He's
1. Lucio and Ana **are not** Brazilian. **They are** from Peru. ______ ______
2. **I am** from Thailand. **I am not** from India. ______ ______
3. **We are** Turkish. We **are not** from Egypt. ______ ______
4. They **are not** Japanese. **They are** from China. ______ ______

3 Look and complete the dialogues.

0
A: Is Paul American?
B: Yes, he is.

1
A: Is Sara from Egypt?
B: No, she ______.

2
A: Are Chris and Drew Australian?
B: Yes, they ______.

Guess What!
It's common to answer *Yes-No* questions with short answers:
✓ Yes, I am. ✗ No, I'm not.
✓ Yes, he is. ✗ No, he isn't.

4 Complete the ID card and describe yourself.

Name

Country

Nationality

______
______
______
______
______

Can

5 Write sentences using *can* or *can't*.

0

jump 3 meters in the air ✓

1

jump 3 meters in the air ✗

2

swim 50 kilometers ✓

3

run 60 km per hour ✓

4

run 60 km per hour ✗

0. Sharks can jump 3 meters in the air.
1. ______________________________
2. ______________________________
3. ______________________________
4. ______________________________

Review

1 Complete the nationality words.

0. In dia n
1. Fr______ch
2. Br______ian
3. Pe______ian
4. It______ian
5. Tu______sh
6. Ja______ese
7. Th______
8. Au______ian
9. Br______sh
10. Eg______ian
11. Gr______k
12. Am______an
13. Ch______ese

2 Read and choose the correct option.

Red Kangaroos

Kangaroos (0) **is** / **are** (circled: are) very common in Australia. They (1) **'s** / **'re** herbivores. Kangaroos (2) **can** / **are** live around 23 years. They (3) **can** / **are** also jump eight meters. Male kangaroos (4) **is** / **are** red. Female kangaroos (5) **is** / **are** gray. Baby kangaroos (6) **can** / **are** called *joeys*. This kangaroo (7) **is** / **can** very big—he (8) **'s** / **'re** two meters tall!

Reading

1 Read and mark (✓). What can you see in Patara?

PATARA

Many **tourists** go to Istanbul, but they can also visit Patara, a famous **beach** in the south of Turkey! The beach is 18 km long! It has Roman ruins, including this ancient **amphitheater**. Many tourists visit Patara to see the wildlife. The area has a lot of birds and turtles. Patara is also a good **destination** for families. It has a **water park** with water slides and swimming pools.

- museums ☐
- the sea ☑
- an airport ☐
- wildlife ☐
- water slides ☐
- ruins ☐

2 Read again and circle *T* (True) or *F* (False).

0. Patara is an island.	T	(F)
1. The beach is very long.	T	F
2. Tourists can visit history museums.	T	F
3. Patara has many birds and turtles.	T	F
4. Patara is not a good place for families.	T	F

Glossary

tourists: visitors from other countries

beach: a sandy place next to the ocean

amphitheater: a structure for watching sports, music or drama performances

destination: a place to visit

water park: an amusement park with water slides and swimming pools

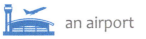

4 Unit

Vocabulary – Rooms and House Objects

1 Look and unscramble.

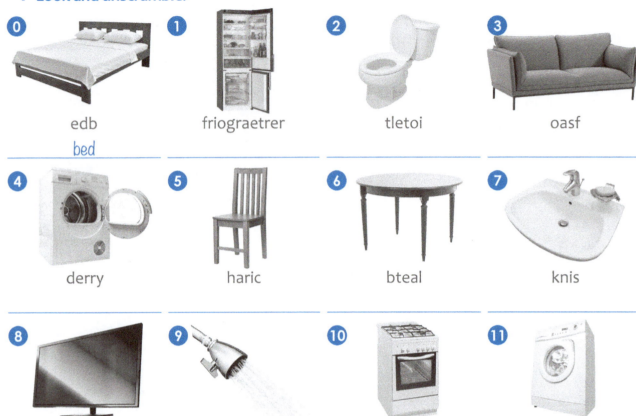

0 
edb
bed

1 
friograetrer

2 
tletoi

3 
oasf

4 
derry

5 
haric

6 
bteal

7 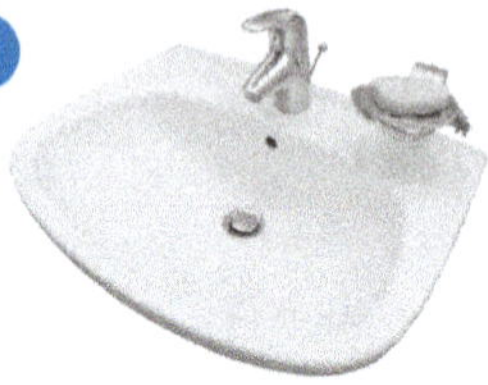
knis

8 
eneltsivio

9 
serohw

10 
sovet

11 
werash

2 Look and label the rooms.

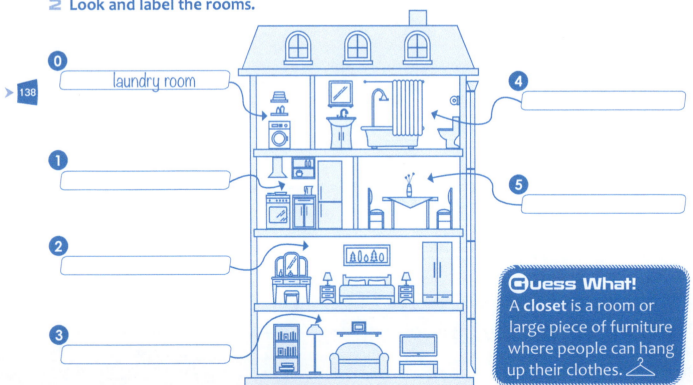

0 laundry room

1 ______

2 ______

3 ______

4 ______

5 ______

Guess What!
A **closet** is a room or large piece of furniture where people can hang up their clothes.

Grammar – *There is* / *There are*

1 Complete the sentences using *'s* or *are*.

0. There _'s_ a TV in the living room.
1. There ______ a table in the kitchen.
2. There ______ three lamps in the dining room.
3. There ______ a lot of photos on the wall.
4. There ______ a sink in the laundry room.

Guess What!
We can add information after sentences with *There is* and *There are*. Use **pronouns** to replace the nouns.
There's **a TV** in the bedroom. **It's** very old.

2 Read and underline. Then match.

0. There are _three cats_ in our house. — They're orange and white.
1. There's a plant in the dining room.
2. There are two chairs in the bedroom.
3. There's a photo of my family in the kitchen.

- It's very special.
- It's very big.
- They're orange and white.
- They're very comfortable.

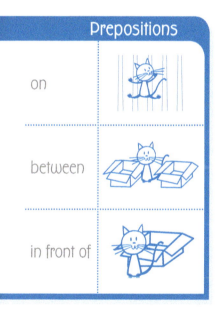

Prepositions

on	
between	
in front of	

3 Look and write the correct preposition.

in front of the sofa

______ the sinks

______ the beds

______ the wall

4 In your notebook, write the negative forms of the sentences.

0. There's a window in the bathroom. _There isn't a window in the bathroom._
1. There's a chair in the laundry room.
2. There are magnets on the fridge.
3. There's a closet in the bedroom.
4. There are books on the table.

5 Write questions. Then look and answer.

0. any plants / the kitchen

   Are there any plants in the kitchen? ✗ No, there aren't.

1. a television / the bedroom

   ______________________ ✗ ______________________

2. magnets / the fridge

   ______________________ ✓ ______________________

3. a lamp / the living room

   ______________________ ✓ ______________________

Short Answers

Is there a plant on the table?
Yes, there **is**.
No, there **isn't**.
Are there (any) plants on the table?
Yes, there **are**.
No, there **aren't**.

6 Complete the questions and answers.

0 Where 's the dog?

It's in the bedroom.

1 Where ____ the magnets?

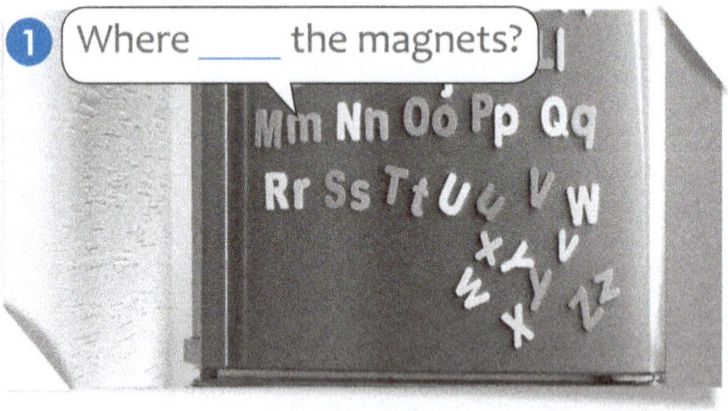

They're ______________________ fridge.

2 Where ____ the dryer?

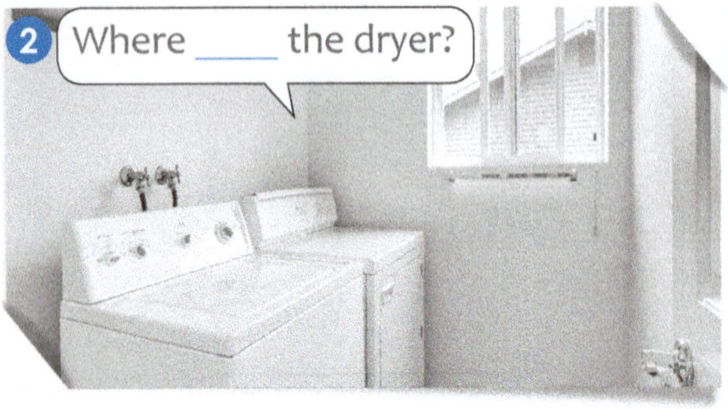

______________________ laundry room.

3 Where ____ the plants?

______________________ living room.

Review

1 In your notebook, correct the sentences.

0. There is two sinks in the bathroom. There are two sinks in the bathroom.
1. There aren't a television in the kitchen.
2. There isn't chairs in the bedroom.
3. Is there a shower in bathroom?
4. Where the photos are?

Reading

1 Read and number the descriptions.

1. cabin

My home is very small. It has one bedroom, one bathroom, a living room and a kitchen. I have some plants on the **balcony**. It's a good place to live because it's modern and it's in the city. ☐

2. mansion

My house is in a **forest**. There are only four rooms: a kitchen, a bedroom, a bathroom and a living room. I have a bed, a desk, a stove and a small fridge. It's not big or modern, but it's **quiet**. ☐

3. apartment

My house is in the countryside. It's big and **luxurious**! It has sixteen bedrooms and ten bathrooms. It also has a movie theater, a gymnasium and a swimming pool. We have great **parties**! ☐

2 Read the descriptions again and complete the table.

big

in a forest

in the city

far from the city

very small

modern

~~not big~~

quiet

luxurious

	Size	Location	Advantages +
1	not big		
2			
3			

Glossary

balcony: an elevated porch area attached to a building

forest: an area with many trees

quiet: silent

luxurious: very elegant and comfortable

parties: (sing. party) fun social events

5 Unit

Vocabulary – Routines

1 Look and complete.

0 

brush my teeth

1 

__________ up

2 

eat __________

3 

get __________

4 

take __________

5 

go to __________

6 

__________ lunch

7 

eat __________

8 

do __________

9 

__________ bed

Time Expressions

2 Look and write the times.

0. 12:00 It's twelve o'clock.
1. 10:30 __________
2. 2:45 __________
3. 9:15 __________
4. 10:05 __________

Guess What!

3:15
It's **a quarter past** three.

3:30
It's **half past** three.

3:45
It's **a quarter to** four.

4:05
It's four **oh** five.

Grammar – Adverbs of Frequency

1 Look and complete using *always, sometimes* or *never.*

0. She ___always___ (✓✓✓✓✓) gets up at eight o'clock.
1. They ____________ (✗✗✗✗✗) go to bed at eleven o'clock.
2. She ____________ (✓✓✗✗✗) plays tennis after school.
3. She ____________ (✓✓✓✓✓) takes a shower at 6:30.
4. He ____________ (✗✓✓✓✓) eats junk food.

2 Write about you.

0. do my English homework
   I always do my English homework.
1. eat junk food
   ____
2. read a book before bed
   ____
3. ride my bike on the weekend
   ____
4. have karate class
   ____

Present Simple

3 Read and complete.

0. Ivan ___doesn't eat___ (not eat) breakfast at 7:45.
1. They ____________ (not take) art classes after school.
2. We ____________ (not do) our homework at night.
3. My grandparents ____________ (not go) to bed at 11 p.m.
4. David ____________ (not eat) lunch at school.
5. My friend ____________ (not go) to the gym on Fridays.

4 Look and write the sentences.

0. Walt / not eat / a big breakfast
   Walt doesn't eat a big breakfast.
1. I / not go to the gym / on Mondays
   ____
2. my friends / play soccer / after school
   ____
3. Carol / eat lunch / eleven o'clock
   ____
4. you / not go to the gym / in the evenings
   ____

5 Complete and match.

0. Do you sleep eight hours? — Yes, I do.
1. Do they ________ to bed at half past nine?
2. ________ Anna do her homework after school?
3. ________ we have karate class on Tuesdays?
4. Does George ________ dinner at seven o'clock?

No, he doesn't.
Yes, she does.
No, they don't.
Yes, I do.
No, we don't.

6 Write the correct form of the verb. Then look and circle the correct option.

0. Jimmy **always** / **sometimes** / **never** wakes up at 6:30 a.m. (wake up)

MONDAY ✓ TUESDAY ✓ WEDNESDAY ✓ THURSDAY ✓ FRIDAY ✓

1. Hamsa **always** / **sometimes** / **never** ________ to bed at 8 o'clock. (go)

MONDAY ✗ TUESDAY ✗ WEDNESDAY ✗ THURSDAY ✗ FRIDAY ✗

2. Joel **always** / **sometimes** / **never** ________ TV in the morning. (watch)

MONDAY ✓ TUESDAY ✗ WEDNESDAY ✗ THURSDAY ✗ FRIDAY ✓

3. Ben **always** / **sometimes** / **never** ________ his homework after dinner. (do)

MONDAY ✓ TUESDAY ✓ WEDNESDAY ✓ THURSDAY ✓ FRIDAY ✓

Review

1 Unscramble the routines.

0. ol tg shcooo — go to school
1. pkew ua ________
2. wd yk oomehmor ________
3. rmhth sy euebt ________
4. nn retdiae ________
5. sohke r wtaae ________

2 Read and circle the correct option.

0. Laura always **take** / **takes** a shower at 7:15.
1. I **don't** / **doesn't** eat junk food.
2. Do you **go** / **goes** to school at 8 o'clock?
3. Max **don't** / **doesn't** eat breakfast before school.
4. **Do** / **Does** Lacy do chores on Saturdays?
5. They **don't** / **doesn't** go to the gym on Fridays.

Guess What!
Most verbs take **–s** with **he**, **she** or **it**.
She sleeps...
She takes...
Other verbs use **–es**...
go → She goes...
do → She does...
watch → She watches
...or **–ies**.
study → She studies...

Reading

1 Classify the activities.

take dance classes · play with my dog · read · watch TV · play soccer · go out with friends · ~~do karate~~ · go to parties · play volleyball · eat pizza

Sports	do karate	
Group Activities		
Other		

2 Read about Rachel and Adrian. Write *R* (Rachel), *A* (Adrian), or *B* (Both).

My Free Time

I'm on the school soccer team and I also do karate. I watch basketball on TV. I always have soccer games on Saturdays. On Sundays, I go out with my friends or go to parties.

I read a lot. I also play volleyball and take dance classes after school. I sometimes play with my dog or watch movies on TV. On Saturdays and Sundays, I go to parties with my friends and eat pizza.

Adrian

Rachel

0. play sports A
1. eat pizza ____
2. watch TV ____
3. read ____
4. go to parties ____
5. play with a dog ____

3 List three things you do in your free time.

____

____

____

Glossary

go out: to go places

Vocabulary – Technology Collocations

1 Circle the verbs.

take photos make phone calls watch movies share photos listen to music check e-mail make a video play games surf the Internet shop online send messages

Guess What!
It's very common to take a photo of yourself —**take a selfie**— to share on social media.

2 Look and label using some of the collocations in Activity 1.

0 
play games

1 
______

2 
______

3 
______

4 
______

5 
______

6 

______

7 
______

8 
______

E-mail

3 Read and complete the e-mail words.

0  d e le te

1  p___i___t

2  ___ep___

3  co___os___

4  ___ve

Grammar – Frequency Expressions

1 Look and complete the sentences.

every day once a week three times a week twice a week

	Mon	Tues	Wed	Thu	Fri	Sat	Sun
	✓			✓			✓
	✓						
						✓	✓
	✓	✓	✓	✓	✓	✓	✓
	✓		✓	✓			

0. Amanda goes to the gym three times a week.
1. She has art class ______________________.
2. She plays tennis ______________________.
3. She listens to music ______________________.
4. She does homework ______________________.

2 Write about Angie using frequency expressions.

0. check e-mail 3 x / day
   Angie checks her e-mail three times a day.
1. shop online 1 x / month
   ____
2. take selfies 2 x / week
   ____
3. surf the Internet M / T / W / TH / F / S / S
   ____
4. listen to music 2 x / day
   ____
5. go to school 5 x / week
   ____
6. share photos 2 x / week
   ____

Guess What!
It is common to use some nouns as verbs:
Call me.
E-mail me.
Text me.

3 In your notebook, answer about you.

How often do you...?

1. text your mom or dad
2. take selfies
3. watch TV
4. read books
5. make videos
6. call your friends

6 Unit

Question Words

4 Read and match.

0. Where do you take photos?	In the morning.
1. What do you watch on TV?	At the park.
2. Who do you text?	Twice a day.
3. When do you listen to music?	My friends and family.
4. How often do you make phone calls?	Sports and movies.

5 Complete using the correct question word.

0 When do you have lunch? — At two o'clock.

1 ________ does Nick watch on TV? — Movies and cartoons.

2 ________ does Ellie text? — Her sister and her mom.

3 ________ do you do homework? — In my bedroom.

4 ________ do your friends share photos? — Every day.

6 Read and complete using the correct forms of the verbs.

call check ~~play~~ send take

0. Where do your cousins play games?
1. When ________ she ________ her e-mail?
2. How often ________ he ________ photos?
3. Who ________ you ________ on your phone?
4. When ________ your brother ________ messages?

Guess What!
Remember that we add *do* or *does* in questions with most verbs. We don't use *do* or *does* in questions with the verb *be*.

Review

1 Write and answer the questions.

0. (? name) What's your name? ________
1. (? favorite color) ________? ________
2. (live) ________? ________
3. (go to bed) ________? ________
4. (play sports) ________? ________
5. (text) ________? ________

Reading

1 Read quickly and circle the correct option.

www.news/summly.com

Summly

NICK D'ALOISIO

Nick Is the **young inventor** of an app called *Summly*. This app helps people who don't have a lot of time. *Summly* creates short **summaries** from long news articles. Each summary is only **a few** sentences. People can read the summaries on the small screens of their phones or tablets. *Summly* is very **successful**. Nick is now a student at Oxford University.

1. What is *Summly*?
   a type of phone / an app
2. Who does *Summly* help?
   children / adults
3. What do people read?
   news articles / books and novels

2 Read again and circle *T* (True) or *F* (False).

0. Nick's app helps people to organize their schedule.	T	(F)
1. The app summarizes information in school books.	T	F
2. Each summary is a few pages long.	T	F
3. People can use the app on tablets.	T	F
4. Nick is a university student.	T	F

Guess What!
Good summaries are short, but they include the important information in a text. They don't include every detail.

3 Read and mark (✓) the best summary of this article.

- ☐ Nick D'Aloisio is the inventor of *Summly*, a successful phone and tablet app.
- ☐ Nick D'Aloisio is a young inventor. He is the inventor of an app called *Summly*. *Summly* makes summaries of news articles for people who don't have a lot of time. It is very successful.
- ☐ Nick is the inventor of an app.

4 List your three favorite apps.

____

____

____

Glossary

young: not old
inventor: a person who creates something new
summaries: (sing. summary) a short form of a text
a few: a small number
successful: popular; with good results

7 Unit

Vocabulary – Clothing

1 Look and label.

blouse boots coat dress hat jacket ~~pajamas~~ pants
scarf ~~scarves~~ ~~shorts~~ skirt ~~socks~~ sweater tie T-shirt

Guess What!

Use *How much is / are the...?* to ask about a price. To reply, say *It's / They're twenty-nine dollars and fifty cents.* or *It's / They're twenty-nine fifty.* ($29.50)

2 Read, find and write the questions.

0. How much are the socks? — They're $9.
1. ______ They're $41.95.
2. ______ It's $125.
3. ______ They're $59.79.
4. ______ It's $12.

Vocabulary – Adjectives

3 Complete the sentences with the correct adjectives.

casual cheap comfortable elegant expensive ~~formal~~ popular useful

0. Is this event formal? Yes, wear a jacket and a tie.
1. These are my favorite pajamas. They're very ________.
2. You look great! Your dress is very ________.
3. Wow! Only $10? These jeans are really ________!
4. On Fridays, we wear ________ clothes to school. I wear jeans.
5. This scarf costs $85. It's very ________!
6. Shorts are ________ for playing sports.
7. Hats are ________ in the winter.

4 Unscramble the sentences.

0. that / an / elegant / is / coat — That is an elegant coat.
1. Henry / has / jacket / an / expensive ________
2. this / is / T-shirt / a / comfortable ________
3. Ugg boots / popular / are / very ________
4. coat / useful / a / the / in / winter / is ________

Grammar – Present Continuous

1 Read and mark (✓) the correct description.

- [ ] Kyle is wearing a shirt, a T-shirt and a pair of jeans. He's also wearing comfortable shoes.
- [ ] Kyle is wearing a shirt, a T-shirt and a pair of pants. He's also wearing black boots.
- [ ] Kyle is wearing a T-shirt and a coat. He's also wearing jeans and black sandals.

2 Read and complete using the correct forms of the verbs.

eat ~~listen~~ sing study take watch

0. Tracy 's listening to music on her tablet.
1. We ________ pizza at the mall.
2. I ________ for an important exam.
3. My brother ________ TV at the moment.
4. Lynn and I ________ selfies with her phone.
5. Mike ________ in the shower!

3 Read and number the lines of the dialogue.

Present Continuous, ?
Are you having lunch?
What is Helen doing?

[1] **OWEN:** Hi there. How are you doing?
[ ] **ANDY:** I'm playing video games.
[ ] **OWEN:** The new James Bond movie. Let's go.
[ ] **ANDY:** Hmm. What's your sister doing? Can she come with us?
[ ] **OWEN:** Fun. I want to go to the movies.
[ ] **ANDY:** What are they showing in the mall?
[ ] **OWEN:** I'm listening to music and reading. You?
[ ] **ANDY:** Oh, hello. I'm fine. What are you doing?

Guess What!
It's common to ask **How are you doing?** as a greeting.
Hi! **How are you doing?**
Fine, thanks.

4 Write questions using the clues. Then number the answers below.

0. (she / study) Is she studying?
1. (they / do homework) ______
2. (what / you / listen to) ______
3. (when / we / have lunch) ______
4. (who / you / talk to) ______
5. (where / we / go) ______

No, they aren't. [ ]   Heavy Metal. [ ]   At 12 o'clock. [ ]
My mom. [ ]   To the mall. [ ]

Review

1 Read and correct the mistakes.

0. I'm wearing a purple ~~jackit~~. jacket
1. These is comfortable pants. ______
2. These are my favorite pijamas. ______
3. That dress is very espensive. ______
4. He wearing a red T-shirt. ______

Reading

1 Look and label.

shorts ______ ______ ______ ______

2 What do these clothes have in common? Read and check your ideas.

In 1871, Jacob Davis and Levi Strauss **produced** denim jeans for miners in California. Denim is a very **durable** and comfortable **material**. Today, people wear denim all over the world. Denim is popular in jackets, skirts and even dresses, but jeans are the most popular. Every year, people buy 1.2 billion pairs of jeans.

Jeans can be blue, **light** blue or even black. The **classic** color for jeans is blue. This color comes from indigo **dye**. Levi is still a **top** producer of jeans, but there are also other companies like Wrangler, Lee and Armani.

3 Read and match.

0. Many clothing items	denim its blue color.
1. Jacob Davis and Levi Strauss	are made from denim.
2. Denim is a useful material because	produced denim jeans for miners.
3. Denim is now popular	also produce jeans.
4. Indigo dye gives	all over the world.
5. Wrangler, Lee and Armani	it is durable.

4 What clothing items does your family have? Make a list in your notebook.

Glossary

produced: the past form of produce (to make)
durable: strong
material: fabric, cloth
light: a color mixed with white
classic: original, typical
dye: a substance that adds color to a material
top: principal

8 Unit

Vocabulary – Vacation Activities

1 Look and complete.

0 
c __ook__ ing

1 
water ________ ing

2 
sh ________ ing

3 
get a t ________

4 
cl ________ ing

5 
sw ________ ing

6 
lift ________ we ________ s

7 
miniature g ________

8 
sn ________ g

9 
su ________ ing

2 Read and complete.

cooking ~~get~~ go (x2) snorkeling play (x2)

Have your next vacation at Newport Island Resort! Sure, you can (0) __get__ a tan by our pool, or (1) ____________ swimming on the beach! You can also go (2) ____________ or saltwater fishing with expert instructors. In the evenings, you can take a (3) ____________ class or practice yoga. We also have excellent sports facilities: you can (4) ____________ tennis, basketball or beach volleyball. Families can (5) ____________ miniature golf or (6) ____________ shopping at the mall next to the resort. See you soon!

Grammar – Likes and Dislikes

1 Look and complete using the correct form of *like, love* or *hate*.

0. We ___like___ going to the gym.
1. Andy ________________ taking photos.
2. I ________________ studying for exams.
3. My friends ________________ watching TV.
4. My mom ________________ going shopping.
5. Kyle ________________ doing chores.

2 Write sentences using the clues.

0. my aunt / love / go to concerts
   My aunt loves going to concerts.
1. Tom and Katie / not like / dance
   ____
2. my grandparents / like / surf the Internet
   ____
3. my brother / hate / wear formal clothing
   ____
4. Lizzy / love / watch movies
   ____
5. my best friend / not like / take selfies
   ____

> **Guess What!**
> We can ask *Yes-No* and *Wh-* questions about likes and dislikes:
> **Do you** like camping? **What do you** love doing?

3 Read and match.

0. What do you like doing? — I like playing the guitar.
1. Do you like playing video games?
2. Does your sister like playing sports?
3. Do your parents like listening to music?
4. Do you like swimming?

No, they don't.
No, I don't.
I like playing the guitar.
Yes, I do. I love playing FIFA.
Yes, she does.

8 Unit

Let's

4 Look and write suggestions using *Let's*.

0.  Let's have lunch.

1. 

____

2.  _______________

3.  _______________

4.  _______________

Review

1 Look and circle the correct option.

0. (go) / play 

1. go / play 

2. go / play 

3. go / play 

4. go / play 

5. go / play 

2 Complete the dialogues using the correct forms of the verbs.

0
- Let's ___go___ (go) shopping.
- I don't like ___going___ (go) shopping. Let's go ___swimming___ (swim).

1
- Does Mike like _______________ (play) soccer?
- No, he _______________.

2
- What do you hate _______________ (do)?
- I hate _______________ (cook).

3
- Do you like _______________ (read)?
- Yes, I love _______________ (read)! Let's _______________ (go) to the library!

3 Answer the questions in your notebook.

1. What do you love doing?
2. What do you hate doing?

Reading

1 Read and label the photos.

bull riding calf roping a lasso rodeo clown

Rodeos are popular in the United States, Canada and parts of Latin America. People love going to rodeos because they are very exciting.

One type of rodeo competition is calf roping. Cowboys ride horses for this activity. They use a *lasso*, or rope, to **catch** a calf.

You can also see **bull** riding. Cowboys sit on large bulls, and the bulls hate it! They jump and try to throw the rider **off**. Bull riding is very dangerous and **injuries** are common.

Did you know there are clowns at many rodeos? When a rider falls off a horse or a bull, rodeo clowns **distract** the animal to protect the rider.

a lasso

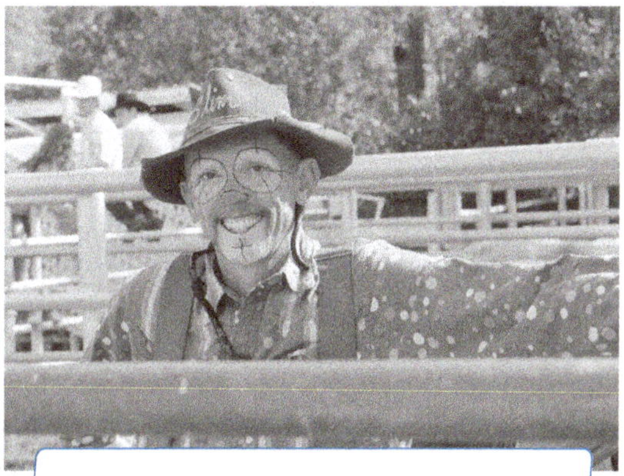

2 In your notebook, compare bull riding and calf roping. How are they similar / different?

Stop and Think! What types of competitions are controversial in your country? Why?

Glossary

catch: to capture

bull: adult male cow

off: not on

injuries: (sing. injury) damage to the body that requires medical treatment

distract: to take attention off of someone or something

Just for Fun Answer Key

Unit 1

1 *Column 1*: MOTHER, FATHER, BROTHER, SISTER, SON, DAUGHTER; *Column 2*: COUSIN, AUNT, UNCLE, GRANDMOTHER, GRANDFATHER; *Secret message*: THERE ARE MANY TYPES OF FAMILIES!

2 1. sister 2. uncle 3. grandmother / grandma

Unit 2

1 1. laboratory 2. gymnasium 3. bathroom 4. computer lab 5. classroom 6. music room

2 *Down*: 1. science 2. history 3. cooking; *Across*: 4. mathematics 5. technology 6. PE 7. geography

Unit 3

1 Australia – 14, Brazil – 3, China – 12, Egypt – 9, France – 5, Greece – 7, India – 11, Italy – 6, Japan – 15, Peru – 2, South Africa – 8, Thailand – 13, Turkey – 10, United Kingdom – 4, United States – 1

2 1. Egypt 2. Brazil 3. Greece 4. Thailand

Unit 4

1 *Down*: 1. chair 2. kitchen 3. washer 4. bathroom 5. bedroom 6. stove; *Across*: 7. dining room 8. fridge 9. living room 10. sofa

2 There's a sink in the bedroom. There's a fridge in the bedroom. There's a stove in the living room. There are toilets in the dining room. There's a sofa in the bathroom.

Unit 5

1 1. I have dinner at half past eight. 2. I take a shower and get dressed at nine p.m. 3. I go to work at ten thirty. 4. I finish work at seven in the morning. 5. I have breakfast at half past seven.

Who am I? a doctor

Unit 6

1 *Down*: 1. compose 2. Internet 3. share 4. check 5. games 6. photos 7. reply 8. online; *Across*: 9. listen 10. print 11. movies 12. delete 13. video 14. message 15. phone 16. save

Unit 7

1 Row 1: sandals, shorts, shoes; Row 2: jeans, boots, pajamas; Row 3: socks, pants; They come in pairs.

2 Sam is wearing a gray sweater. Charlie is wearing a blue T-shirt. Jess is wearing red shoes. Anna is wearing brown boots.

Unit 8

1 1. miniature golf 2. shopping 3. snorkeling 4. weights 5. tan 6. surfing 7. cooking classes 8. climbing 9. swimming 10. waterskiing

2 1. play miniature golf 2. go shopping 3. go snorkeling 4. lift weights 5. get a tan 6. go surfing 7. take cooking classes 8. go climbing 9. go swimming 10. go waterskiing

Grammar Reference

Demonstratives

We use demonstratives to indicate a specific item or group of items. There are different forms for singular or plural and near or far.

- ***This*** *is my brother.*
- ***That*** *is my sister.*
- ***These*** *are my cats.*
- ***Those*** *are my grandparents.*

We also use demonstratives before nouns: ***this*** *flower*, ***that*** *star*.

Possessive Adjectives

We use possessive adjectives before nouns to show the relationship between that noun and a person.

- *Karen is* ***my*** *mother.*
- *Michelle is* ***her*** *sister.*

We use them to show something belongs to somebody.

- *This is* ***my*** *house.*

Each possessive adjective is related to a subject pronoun.
I / my; you / your; he / his; she / her; it / its; we / our; they / their.

Possessive *'s*

We use the possessive *'s* to show possession.

- *Michelle is Karen****'s*** *sister.*
- *Peter is Lisa****'s*** *cousin.*
- *That is Tom****'s*** *book.*

Verb *be*

We use the verb *be* to describe the characteristics or a person, thing or idea.

- *This* ***is*** *my dad.*
- *His name* ***is*** *James.*

We use the form *am* with the subject *I*.

- *I* ***am*** *Sally.*

We use the form *is* with the subjects *he*, *she* and *it*.

- *Sue* ***is*** *my cousin.*
- *He* ***is*** *my uncle.*
- *It* ***is*** *my dog.*

We use *are* with the subjects *you*, *we* and *they*.

- *Max and Simon* ***are*** *my cousins.*
- *You* ***are*** *12 years old.*
- *We* ***are*** *cousins.*

When we make *Yes/No* questions, we put the verb *be* before the subject.

- ***Is*** *Amy your sister?*
- ***Are*** *those your neighbors?*

Indefinite Articles

Indefinite articles come before nouns.

- *I have **a** pencil.*

We use *a* before words that begin with a consonant sound. We use *an* before words that begin with a vowel sound.

- *I have **a** notebook.* (consonant sound)
- *I have **an** eraser.* (vowel sound)

Note that the sound—not the spelling—of the noun is important.

- *I have **an** mp3 player.* (vowel sound, consonant spelling)
- *He is **a** university student.* (consonant sound, vowel spelling)

We also use indefinite articles before occupations.

- *She is **a** teacher.*

Verb *have*

We use *have* to talk about relationships, possessions and scheduled activities.

- *I **have** two brothers.*
- *I **have** a tablet in my backpack.*
- *I **have** math class in the morning.*

We use *have* with *I, you, we* and *they*.

- *We **have** chemistry in the afternoon.*

We use *has* with *he, she* and *it*.

- *Amanda **has** P.E. in the morning.*

We use *don't (do not)* and *doesn't (does not)* with *have* for negative sentences. We use *don't have* with *I, you, we* and *they*.

- *We **don't have** music class in the auditorium.*

We use *doesn't have* with *he, she* and *it*.

- *Carl **doesn't have** art class this year.*

To form *Yes/No* questions, we put *do* or *does* before the subject.

- ***Do** you **have** an extra pencil?*
- ***Does** it **have** an eraser?*

We answer *Yes/No* questions with short answers.

- ***Do** you have a pencil? **Yes, I do.***
- ***Does** it have an eraser? **No, it doesn't.***

Prepositions

We use the prepositions *in, on, under* and *next to* to describe the location of objects.

- *My calculator is **in** my backpack.*
- *My notebook is **on** the desk.*
- *The pencil is **next to** the notebook.*
- *My backpack is **under** the chair.*

Verb *be*

The verb *be* can also be used in contractions *I'm (I am), You're (You are), She's (She is), We're (We are),* and *They're (They are).*

- *She**'s** American.*
- *They**'re** French.*

We also form contractions using *be* and not to express negation: *You aren't (are not), He isn't (is not), We aren't (are not), They aren't (are not).*

- *He **isn't** Australian.*
- *We **aren't** Japanese.*

Can

We use the modal *can* to express ability. The negative form is *can't*. The form is the same for all subjects.

- *I **can** dance.*
- *My sister **can** swim.*
- *Turtles **can't** jump.*

To form *Yes/No* questions, we put *can* before the subject.

- ***Can** polar bears climb trees?*

We form short answers using the subject and *can*.

- ***Can** he dance? Yes, he **can**. / No, he **can't**.*

There is / There are

We use *There is* and *There are* to say that something exists. The contracted form of *There is* is *There's*.

- ***There's** a sofa in the living room.*

There are is the plural form.

- ***There are** four chairs in the dining room.*

The negative forms are *There isn't* (*is not*) and *There aren't* (*are not*). It is common to use *any* with the plural form.

- ***There isn't** a table in the dining room.*
- ***There aren't** any lamps in the bedroom.*

To form *Yes/No* questions, we put the verb *be* before *there*.

- ***Is there** a plant in the bathroom?*
- ***Are there** plants in the kitchen?*

These are the short answer forms:

- *Yes, **there is**. / No, **there isn't**.*
- *Yes, **there are**. / No, **there aren't**.*

Where

Where is a question word. We use questions with *where* to ask about the location of places and objects.

- ***Where** is the sofa?*

Prepositions

We use the prepositions *on*, *between* and *in front of* to describe the location of objects.

- *There are photos **on** the wall.*
- *The chair is **between** two lamps.*
- *The table is **in front of** the window.*

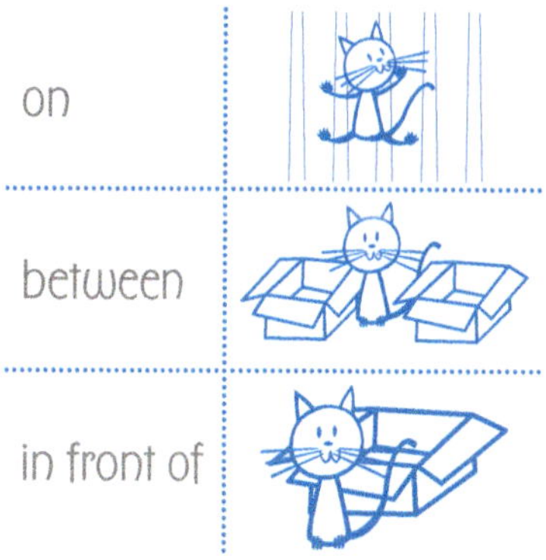

Adverbs of Frequency

An adverb is a word that modifies a verb. We use adverbs of frequency to express how often an activity takes place.

The most common adverbs of frequency are *always*, *sometimes* and *never*. *Always* means that an activity occurs all the time. *Sometimes* means that an activity occurs occasionally but not all the time. *Never* is the opposite of *always*. It means that an activity does not occur at all.

- *I **always** eat breakfast in the morning.*
- *I **sometimes** eat a snack after school.*
- *I **never** eat after eight o'clock.*

Adverbs of frequency appear before most verbs, but after the verb *be*.

- *William **always** studies for exams.*
- *He is **always** a good student.*

Present Simple

We use the present simple to talk about permanent states and routines. We use the base form of the verb with *I*, *you*, *we* and *they*.

- *I **wake** up at six o'clock.*

We use the third person singular form with *he*, *she* and *it*. To make verbs in the third person, we add *–s* or *–es* to the base form of the verb.

- *She wake**s** up at six thirty.*
- *He watch**es** TV in the afternoon.*

Verbs take *–es* when the verb ends in *–ss*, *–x*, *–ch*, *–sh*, or *–o*. This is only for third person singular subjects.

- *Mr. Reed teach**es** math.*
- *Paula go**es** to the gym on Tuesdays.*

When a verb ends in consonant + *–y*, we change the *–y* to *–i* and add *–es*.

- *Glen **studies** at the library on Sundays.*

Verbs with the subjects *I*, *you*, *we* and *they* do not change.

- *I **study** on Wednesdays.*
- *We **go** to the park on Saturdays.*

To form negative sentences, we use *don't* or *doesn't* with the base form of the verb. We use *don't* for *I*, *you*, *we* and *they*.

- *I **don't eat** junk food for dinner.*
- *They **don't have** karate class on Mondays.*

We use *doesn't* for third person singular subjects (*he*, *she*, *it*).

- *She **doesn't watch** TV in the morning.*
- *He **doesn't eat** lunch at 2 p.m.*

To form *Yes*/*No* questions in the present simple, we use *do* or *does* before the subject. We use *do* for the subjects *I*, *you*, *we* and *they*. We use *does* for *he*, *she* and *it*.

- ***Do** they go to the gym on Fridays?*
- ***Does** Ms. Harrold **teach** chemistry?*

Short answers include the subject and the affirmative or negative form of *do* or *does*.

- *Yes, they **do**. / No, they **don't**.*
- *Yes, she **does**. / No, she **doesn't**.*

Frequency Expressions

We use frequency expressions to express how often an activity occurs in a specific period of time (for example, the number of times in a day, in a week, in a month, in a year).

- *Jason checks his e-mail* ***three times a day****.*
- *He takes photos* ***three times a week****.*

We use *once* to mean *one time*. We use *twice* to mean *two times*.

- *Emily watches movies* ***once*** *a week.*
- *She makes phone calls* ***twice*** *a day.*

We can also say *every* to indicate all days / weeks / months, etc.

- *We study English* ***every*** *day.*
- *I have music class* ***every*** *week.*

Question Words

There are different question words for different types of information. The most common question words are *What, Where, Who* and *When. How* is also a question word. We use it in this unit to ask *How often*.

We use *What* to ask for general information.

- ***What*** *is your name?*
  Janice.
- ***What*** *is your favorite app?*
  Instagram.

We use *Where* to ask about a place.

- ***Where*** *do you study?*
  In the dining room.

We use *Who* to ask about people.

- ***Who*** *sends you messages?*
  My friends and my mom.

We use *When* to ask about times.

- ***When*** *do you study?*
  After school.

We use *How often* to ask about the frequency of activities.

- ***How often*** *do you use your phone?*
  Every day.

Present Continuous

We use the present continuous to talk about activities that are happening now. We form the present continuous with the verb *be* in the present simple, and the base form of the verb with *-ing*.

- *I **am listening** to music.*
- *We **are watching** TV.*

The contracted form is more common.

- ***I'm listening**.*
- ***We're watching** TV.*

Some verbs require spelling changes. We double the consonant in verbs with a short vowel sound that end in a consonant.

- *We're **sitting** on the sofa. (sit)*

We remove the *–e* and add *–ing* to verbs with a long vowel that end in *–e*.

- *They're **taking** photos at the park.*

We form the negative by adding *not* after the verb be.

- *She is **not** exercising.*
- *They are **not** eating lunch.*

Most people use the contracted form.

- *She **isn't** exercising.*
- *They **aren't** eating lunch.*

To form *Yes/No* questions, we put the verb *be* before the subject. We don't use the main verb in short answers.

- ***Is** he **studying**?*
  Yes, he ***is***. / No, he ***isn't***.

Likes and Dislikes

We talk about likes and dislikes by using the words *love, like, don't/doesn't like* and *hate*.

Likes and Dislikes

love 

like 

don't / doesn't like 

hate 

After *love, like* or *hate*, we use a main verb with an *–ing* ending.

- *I **love** read**ing**.*
- *She **doesn't like** watch**ing** TV.*

To form *Yes/No* questions, we add *Do* or *Does* before the subject.

- ***Do** you **love** read**ing**?*
  Yes, I do. / No, I don't.
- ***Does** she **like** watch**ing** TV?*
  Yes, she does. / No, she doesn't.

We form *Wh–* questions by adding a question word before *do* or *does*.

- ***What** do you love doing?*

Verbs with *–ing* endings have spelling changes as with the present continuous.

- *We love **swimming**.* (double consonant)
- *He likes **taking** photos.* (remove *–e*)

Let's

We use *Let's* with a verb in the base form to offer suggestions for activities. *Let's* is short for *Let us*. It means *We should do something*.

- ***Let's go** to the park!*
- ***Let's have** lunch!*

Verb List

Base Form	Present Simple: 3rd Person Singular	Verb + *–ing*
be	**is**[1]	being
brush	**brushes**[2]	brushing
call	calls	calling
check	checks	checking
circle	circles	**circling**[4]
climb	climbs	climbing
compose	composes	**composing**[4]
cook	cooks	cooking
dance	dances	**dancing**[4]
delete	deletes	**deleting**[4]
do	**does**[2]	doing
eat	eats	eating
e-mail	e-mails	e-mailing
exercise	exercises	**exercising**[4]
get	gets	**getting**[5]
go	**goes**[2]	going
have	**has**[1]	**having**[4]
jump	jumps	jumping
lift	lifts	lifting
listen to	listens to	listening to
live	lives	**living**[4]
look	looks	looking
make	makes	**making**[4]
open	opens	opening
play	plays	playing
print	prints	printing
read	reads	reading
relax	**relaxes**[2]	relaxing
reply	**replies**[3]	replying
save	saves	**saving**[4]
send	sends	sending
share	shares	**sharing**[4]
shop	shops	**shopping**[5]
sit	sits	**sitting**[5]
sleep	sleeps	sleeping
study	**studies**[3]	studying
surf	surfs	surfing
swim	swims	**swimming**[5]
take	takes	**taking**[4]
text	texts	texting
use	uses	**using**[4]
wake up	wakes up	**waking**[4] **up**
watch	**watches**[2]	watching
wear	wears	wearing
write	writes	**writing**[4]

[1] These are irregular verbs. [2] Add *–es* with third person singular.
[3] The *–y* becomes *–ies* with third person singular. [4] The *–e* is removed in verb + *–ing*.
[5] The consonant doubles in verb + *–ing*.